Pike And Perch Fishing: Being A Practical Treatise On Angling With Float, Paternoster, And Leger, In Still Water And Stream

John William Martin

PIKE AND PERCH FISHING.

BEING A PRACTICAL TREATISE ON ANGLING WITH FLOAT,
PATERNOSTER, AND LEGER, IN STILL WATER
AND STREAM.

*INCLUDING CHAPTERS ON SPINNING WITH NATURAL
AND ARTIFICIAL BAITS, AND ALSO LIVE
AND DEAD GORGING.*

By J. W. MARTIN,

THE "TRENT OTTER."

*A Working Man Angler's Experiences; written expressly for the
benefit of his brethren of the Craft.*

WITH ILLUSTRATIONS.

ALL RIGHTS RESERVED.

PUBLISHED BY
THE ANGLER, LIMITED, AT THE OFFICES, SCARBOROUGH.
1898.

Prefatory Introduction

My Dear Brother Fishermen, — The two small companion volumes that I had the honour and pleasure of introducing to you about a year ago, have been received with considerable success. I am deeply grateful to you all for your kindness, and wish now to still further increase my obligations in that respect. To this end I beg to introduce to your, I hope, favourable consideration, the present little effort of my pen, which is part 4, vol. 3, of the series ; and which I entitle, "Pike and Perch Fishing."

This book is not intended sole *y* for the benefit of well-to-do pike fishermen, who can travel far and wide for their sport, and who have the very best private waters in the kingdom at their disposal; and plenty of money to purchase any and every pike tackle and artificial that takes their fancy. It is rather the working man angler, who has few opportunities to wet his line in well-stocked private lakes and rivers, that I am more particularly addressing in the following pages.

The latter class of angler is extremely anxious to have put before him the simplest and most inexpensive method that can be adopted in well-fished public waters. His pockets have not much of a golden lining, and if he can successfully ply his craft at an expenditure of only a few shillings, he will like it far better than if a whole host of things were set before him and most strongly recommended.

To this end I have brought my own experiences as a working man angler, who has had to toil in factory and farmyard, to bear; and have given what I consider to be the simplest and most effective methods to adopt in all conditions of pike and perch fishing, that the ordinary working man will have placed at his disposal.

This question was once summed up neatly by a journey-man sweep, who one day was spinning a likely-looking stretch of the Trent; his attention had been called to a paragraph in one of the sporting papers, in which it was stated that "Mr. S, fishing Lord B's private lake, had succeeded in landing a splendid bag of large pike." "Ah," said our friend the sweep, at the same time jerking his head in the direction of a woman and two children sitting on the bank, "If Mr. S., the noted pike slayer, was on this, or any other well-fished public water, and had his wife and two kids sitting on the bank, waiting while he caught a jack, which had also to be sold before a bit of bread could be procured for their breakfasts, same as they are waiting for over yonder, I reckon his bags would not be much heavier than the rest of us anglers are." I hope none of my readers will be so hard up as to depend for their breakfasts on the fish they catch, but the little inci-dent is useful in illustrating my meaning.

Personally I don't pretend to have any literary ability. What I have written is only a plain statement of fact, and written as one old worker would write to his mates. Neither do I pretend to be a better fisherman than hundreds more that are found in almost any big town and city in England. I know just enough to amuse myself, but I do claim to be an observant angler ; one who notes any strange thing that comes his way, and who does not rest contented until he has reasoned out for himself the why and wherefore of it. Added to this, I have had peculiar advantages that does not come within reach of the generality of my poorer brethren. I have been an angler from my earliest boyhood, and constantly thrown in the society of men who are angling gems of the very first water.

These are a few of the considerations that prompt me to hope for a favourable reception at your hands, of this little volume. I won't promise you an elaborately illustrated, and finely got-up book, but I will promise you a most carefully written, and at the same time plain essay on pike and perch fishing, so that the veriest novice will not stumble during his journey through its pages. For I have taken the liberty of assuming that some of you are novices pure and simple, who know next to nothing on the subject here specially treated.

The principles I lay down are the principles of economy, coupled with the most effective results that a lifetime's experience has suggested and studied from many and various standpoints. I also dedicate this volume to my fellow working men anglers, and ask them to treat it and me as favourably as they can.

1898.   JOHN WM. MARTIN,
                               " The Trent Otter."

CONTENTS.

PART IV.—PIKE AND PERCH.

THE PIKE.

CHAPTER I.

THE PIKE AND HIS CHARACTERISTICS.

Ancient writers on the pike—Description of the pike—His habits—His ferocity and voracity—Tench as food or doctor—The haunts of pike—Jack in a baited swim—Weight and growth of pike—Jack fishing in public waters, a contrast—The first English writer on pike and pike fishing—The gander and the pike—Pike in ancient times—Pike on the table—Different methods of jack fishing.

> " He loves no streams, but hugs the silent deeps,
> And eats all hours, and yet no house he keeps."

So sang Theophilus Franck a good many years ago, when writing of "that mercenary, the lucit or pike." And all writers, both in prose and poetry, that have taken this fish as a text, are pretty well agreed in the general character they give him. They looked upon his formidable teeth, his wicked eyes, and his villainous aspect as being quite sufficient to inspire any amount of terrible description ; even the very look and sound of his name they found to be suggestive of voracity and ferocity. Indeed, the very first writer who mentions the pike—viz., the Latin poet Ausonius, who, writing about the fourth century—says,

> " The wary Luce, 'midst wrack and rushes hid,
> The scourge and terror of the scaly brood."

and Pope, too, sings of him in much the same strains when he says,

> " And pikes, the tyrants of the watery plains."

" The Innocent Epicure," written about the year 1697, contains the following lines :

> " Go on, my muse, next let thy numbers speak
> That mighty Nimrod of the streams, the pike."

These two or three examples go to prove that even old

B

writers, when trolling for pike was very little known, or at most only in its infancy, regarded the pike as a fish of character preying upon his smaller and weaker kindred; while the very look of his powerful and cruel jaws they held to be sufficient to strike terror into the hearts of the timid and superstitious people of those days.

Years ago, when I only had what I could claim as a very rudimentary knowledge of this fish and his habits, I used to eagerly read everything connected with him that I could possibly get hold of, and, like a true enthusiast, believe it all; and the more wild and improbable the story, the greater was my belief. But viewed nowadays, by the cold light of several years' practical experience, I am sadly afraid that there have been more lies—to put it in very plain English—told about our pike than are exactly good for his character and reputation. For instance, look at that tale that is mentioned, I should suppose, in dozens of books on angling and natural history, about that giant pike, said to have been captured in 1497, out of a lake in the vicinity of Manheim, which legend or tradition said had a medal fastened to one of his gills with an inscription saying it had been turned into the lake by Frederick the Second in the year 1232! It would appear from this that that pike had lived over 250 years, and had survived many social and political changes. But the most astounding part of this fish fable was not exactly its Old Parr-like antiquity, but the giant size it was said to have attained, being no less than 19ft. in length, and reaching a weight of 350 lb.; and then to prove the statement they tell us that his skeleton could be seen by anyone interested, as it is, or was, carefully preserved in the Manheim Museum; but unfortunately on a careful examination of this skeleton by a naturalist, he came to the conclusion that it was a clever deception, and had evidently been built up for the occasion.

Our English pike, or jack, as it is generally called nowadays, when in good condition is a handsome fish, and a fish that is much sought after by anglers of all degrees. I know of no other fish for whose capture such a bewildering quantity of artificial baits, spinning tackles and flights, live-bait tackles, floats, and traces have been invented.

The scientific name of the pike is " Esox Lucius," and on looking up a dictionary I find he is described thus:—" So called from the shape of his head and jaws. Head depressed, large, oblong, blunt; jaws, palatine bones and vomer furnished with teeth of various sizes; body, elongated, rounded on the back, sides compressed, covered with scales; dorsal fin placed far back over the anal fin; whole body mottled with white, yellow, and green." Walton calls the pike "a solitary, melancholy, and bold fish," and certainly this is a very good description, although some odd times they may be found congregated together in considerable numbers; but speaking generally they are not very often discovered in shoals like roach, dace, and bream; more often than not, especially during the winter months, are they solitary tenants of a quiet reedy corner, away from the rush of the main stream, sole monarchs of that small domain, ready to pounce out at a moment's notice on any unwary roach or dace that happens to stray within striking distance. One writer describing the habits and haunts of the pike uses a few sentences that are worth repeating, he says: " Shrouded from observation in his solitary retreat, he follows with his eye the shoals of fish that wander heedlessly along; he marks the water-rat swimming to his burrow, the ducklings paddling among the water-weeds, the dabchick and the moor-hen swimming leisurely on the surface; he selects his victim, and like the tiger springing from the jungle he rushes forth, seldom missing his aim; there is a sudden swirl and splash, circle after circle forms on the surface of the water, and all is still again in an instant." A long catalogue of fables and traditions have been handed down from one writer to another on this point of our jack's savage ferocity, and also on his marvellous powers of digestion; and none of these traditions seem to lose anything by being repeated, and I don't know that they need, for he has well earned that name given him by certain writers—the "freshwater shark." What he won't take as a bait would be rather a more difficult question to answer than what he will, for there are hundreds of anecdotes told about him, and the astounding things he will seize at a pinch. One writer says " that a swan was once noticed on a lake with its

head and neck under the water; the circumstances seemed
so peculiar that a boat was procured, and on proceeding to
the spot it was discovered that a pike had swallowed the
head of the swan, which was firmly fixed in his throat, and
being unable to extricate themselves from this extraordinary
difficulty the pair of them were dead." I should not suppose
the pike opened his ponderous jaws with intent to swallow
the swan altogether; perhaps he only saw the head and neck
deep down in the water, and had not noticed the body
attached. Anyhow, for once in a way he had made a fatal
mistake. Another anecdote mentions a pike seizing the lips
of a mule that had gone to the edge of the lake to drink;
and still another historian puts on record that a pike
seized the foot of a Polish woman who had stepped into a
stream. But we can hardly take these statements seriously,
for, personally, when I have got into close quarters with
pike, and peered ever so cautiously through the flags and
rushes at them, as soon as ever my eyes met the wicked-
looking ones of the fish, like a flash of light he would vanish,
and leave scarcely a ripple behind. Once, however, I saw
a 4lb. jack maul the hand of a keeper badly, and the
strangest part of the story was that the jack had been out
of the water nearly two hours. After packing up the rods
and tackle, the keeper threw the fish out of the boat on to
the grassy bank, and some few minutes afterwards stooped
down to pick it up again, when, to our utter astonishment,
as soon as his hand neared the jack it made a sudden grab
and seized him by the thick part of his thumb, inflicting
some nasty cuts, which were weeks before they healed up.
The keeper said he was served the same trick once before,
only that time he had got the fish home, and was going to
remove them from a pump trough after washing, when one
collared him in the same way. This was the painful experience of Harry Rout, the then keeper of the Huntingdon
Angling Society's water, and the memory of that wounded
hand haunts me to this day, and causes me to impress most
strongly on the young pike fisher that on no account must
he put his hands too near the jaws of a jack, for if he does
get operated on with those horrible teeth, he will most likely
remember it for the rest of his natural life. Be very careful

in disengaging hooks from pike.   Always carry a short
heavy bludgeon, and as soon as Mr. Jack is safely landed,
hit him two or three smart raps fair between the eyes; this
will effectually stun him and cause him to widely open his
mouth, when the hooks can be poked out with a long
disgorger. But I must get back to my text. It has also
been put on record that the body of a child was once found
in the stomach of a pike.   I have never found anything so
strange as that in any of the jack I have opened; but rats,
chickens, young ducks, moor-hens, and fish of various kinds
I have often discovered.   Pike have been known to get
themselves in strange difficulties, and no possible chance of
extricating themselves; but I should question if ever a pair
of them were in a queerer fix than the two exhibited in the
South Kensington Museum.   These two jack, that weighed
together about 19lb., and nearly of the same size, are firmly
fixed together, the head of one, up to the termination of
the gills, being tight in the throat of the other.   A boatman
saw them struggling together in Loch Tay, locked in each
other's jaws, and promptly gaffed them, sending them to Mr.
Buckland without being separated, who took a cast of them.
We can only wonder what these fish were doing—fighting,
perhaps. I should not suppose that one of them opened his
mouth with the deliberate intention of swallowing the other,
for they are both of a size, unless one of them was suffering
from some curious deformity of vision.   In Sweden, the land
of enormous perch and pike, it is no infrequent occurrence
for very large perch to swallow the baited hooks of stationary night-lines, and then for pike in their turn to swallow the
hooked perch.   In this case, though the pike himself is
hardly ever hooked, yet the perch, with the help of his
spiked fins and hard scales, sets so fast in the throat of the
greedy tyrant that he is unable to get rid of it, and both are
taken.   Pike when hungry will seize almost anything that is
moving in the water which bears the least resemblance to a
small fish, a rat, or a young moor-hen; but when he is not
on the feed hardly anything will tempt him.   Expert pike
fishers know very well the difference between the " runs," as
they are called, when he is hungry, and when he is not.
When not hungry he will often play with a bait; and have

no intention of taking it fairly so that he can be hooked. He will often allow himself to be hauled about, and even dragged up to the surface of the water, only, with a flap of his tail, to drop the bait from his jaws, and roll over again into the deep water; and you could almost fancy there was a mocking grin during the process on his villainous looking face. I think it is a good job that the pike are more often off the feed than on, because if they were always hungry there would, in waters were they are plentiful and carefully preserved, be nothing else left with them either alive or dead, for most assuredly everything else that could be eaten would be speedily cleared out; for one authority tells us that a jack when on the feed will eat his own weight in gudgeons and other small fish in the course of a few days. The Rev. Mr. Manley, a gifted writer on the habits and history of our fresh water fishes, says of the pike, "that in reality nothing comes amiss to him. He has no more taste, in the true sense of the word, than he has feeling. All's fish, at least food, that comes into his net. Certainly when left to his natural devices he is a sort of gentleman who would eat the toast on which asparagus is placed to drain, the tinfoil in which Rochefort cheese is enwrapped, the crust of a game pie, or the envelopment of an Oxford brawn. The only wonder is how he can manage to live at all in certain waters. The truth is he is endowed with the power of long fasting, which doubtless he often exercises, either from necessity or choice." But in spite of his great voracity, there are certain things that he does not care much about; he does not like a toad, though he is dearly fond of a frog. It has also been said that he will have nothing to do with a perch; perhaps he may not care about them much, and would pass them by if plenty of other food existed in the water, but I knew one very large pond in the county of Lincoln, that contained nothing else, as far as we could make out, except jack, perch, eels, and a few tench; and yet a small perch about the length of your finger was the only bait, except an occasional frog, that was any use at all to the pike of that water. And then again we hear that he won't have anything to do with a tench; but I knew a gentleman who brought down to a well known pike water a can of small

tench, carp, and gold fish, and got half-a-dozen right good
jack with the tench as bait; and strange as it may seem,
not a single run did he get with the much more brilliant
gold fish. Izaak Walton says on this point that " the tench
is the physician of fishes, for the pike especially, who for-
bears to devour him, be he never so hungry." Other old
writers have also strongly endorsed this opinion; saying
that the slime or touch of tenches, was a certain cure for
wounds, cuts, or ailments in the fishy tribe generally; and
the pike more particularly. But I am sadly afraid this is
only an old legend that has not much solid foundation in
fact. If it was true, and our jack could reason for himself
like a human being, he might spare him, for no man who is
in possession of his senses would want to swallow his doctor.
I also read some time ago, that a quantity of tench were
turned into a lake that contained a lot of ill-conditioned pike
as an experiment, and some time afterwards the pike improved to a remarkable extent! but it did not state positively
if this result was due to simply the presence of the tench
in the water, or whether the increase of condition was due
to the supply of fresh food, that was so generously and
plentifully at hand in the shape of that stock of tench. The
writer rather hinted that he thought it was entirely due to
simply the presence of the tench in the water. I am also
afraid that this statement is not worth much, for I knew a
sheet of water in Nottinghamshire that contained a large
quantity of very fine tench, but the few jack that shared
the water with them were the ugliest and most ill-conditioned
brutes we ever caught. I fancy that for pike to be in good
condition depends more on the water they inhabit, and the
abundance of natural food in the water with them, than
just turning a few tench in. I don't believe that turning a
hundred or two of tench in a real bad jack water will improve the breed and condition of the latter to any permanent
extent. As I said a little while ago, the pike, generally
speaking, is a solitary fish, though large ones are often found
in pairs. After floods and frosts, or owing to some
accidental circumstances, they may sometimes be found
collected together in numbers in favourable eddies, or in a
backwater away from the main stream, or at the tail end of

an island where the stream is, as it were, cut in two, with a considerable quiet eddy between those two streams. By the side of reed beds, among flags and rushes, in corners and lay-byes, at the tail ends of old lochs, up deepish backwaters, or a cutting that has an entrance into the river. A deepish corner away from the main stream, particularly if it is fringed along the edge with a dense undergrowth of weeds, and water-lilies, with a scattered crop of flags and rushes here and there, is, generally speaking, a capital spot in which to find pike. Sometimes very good ones are met with in the rough water close under a weir, more particularly if some very large stones stick up above the surface of the water, and a deep eddy is formed at the back, in which the frothing waters keep churning round and round. I have taken some very good jack from similar situations; once in particular I got an eight-pounder with a spoon bait, from close under the foot of a weir, in an eddy barely six feet by three, and not more than two feet deep, that was formed by an old tree root that had been swept over the weirs. In swift running rivers like the Trent it is only occasionally that they are met with in midstream where the current is strong, preferring to hug the shore, particularly if that shore has an overhanging bank, and is thickly fringed with willow boughs, weeds, and flags. If they are found out in the main stream, it is generally at a very deep bend, where the water does not race along at such speed as it does over the shallows; at these places during the early autumn good jack are often picked up by knowing anglers, who sink a spinning bait deep down in midstream, and slowly wind it home. In slow running rivers like the Bedfordshire Ouse, it does not so particularly matter selecting the deepest corners; indeed, during the late summer and early autumn the shallows and weedy places, over which a slight stream wanders along, even if less than a yard in depth, and the spinning bait has to be so manipulated that it must not, for fear of catching the weeds, be allowed to sink even three inches under the surface, are by far the best places to try. During the winter when the weather is cold and frosty, the deeps can be tried with more chance of success; although this is not a hard and fast rule, as I have taken good pike from very shallow

water in the Ouse, when the weather has been very severe
indeed, but still taking it all round, the deeps show the
best results when the weather is very cold. As for good
pike lakes; these are generally preserved and protected to
such an extent, that the average working-man-angler does not
get many chances to wet a line in them. It is not such a
difficult matter to find out the haunts of pike in lakes, as it
is in rivers; although I am aware that even in the circum-
scribed space of a small pike lake, those fish have their
favourite haunts, some places being tenanted very thickly,
while other parts would have next to nothing in them. I
remember once going with a gentleman to fish a small lake
of some four or five acres, in which he had been given to
understand were a lot of good jack; we wandered three
parts of the way round that pond trying all likely and even
unlikely places, but never saw a pike move, until at last we
came to the opposite corner, within fifty yards from where
we started, and there we found the home of those fish.
I should say that fully nine-tenths of the pike in that lake
were in a good deal less than half-an-acre of water. Sometimes when the bottom fisherman has groundbaited a swim
in a river some considerable time, and has been enjoying
capital sport, the fish suddenly go off the feed. It is quite
likely under the circumstances, if the water contains pike,
that several of those customers have been attracted into the
swim, putting the other fish off the feed, if not exactly scar-
ing them away altogether. Some of the very best bags of
jack I can remember, have been taken under these circumstances; some lively dace have been procured, fixed on snap
tackle, and run down the whole of the swim, which resulted
in the baited bream swim, or whatever it was, being cleared
of those pike, and the sport among the other fish recom-
menced. I heard the late Jim Chatterton once say, that a
friend and himself took thirteen in one afternoon ranging
from two to ten pounds each, out of a barbel swim in the
Corporation Fishery on the Trent, after they had tried for
two days without result to catch the fish they baited the
place for. It suddenly struck him that the pike had taken
possession, because they had been having such good sport
among the dace, roach, chub, and bream, a few days before.

A trial proved this theory to be correct. I could select from my own experiences several more instances of the same kind, but I have said enough I think to give our young fisherman a useful hint. Pike spawn between the latter end of February and the end of April, or even under exceptional circumstances right to the middle of May, but it all depends on the state of the weather, as to whether they are early or late. I have noticed them pairing as early as February and in the same season observed them even as late as the second week in May; in fact, I have an idea that it is a long and trying time for them. During this operation they seek all sorts of dykes, ditches, creeks, and backwaters, depositing the ova among the weeds, and so lazy and absorbed are they, that scarcely anything will frighten them. Scores of them have been lifted out with wire snares, or even scooped out with landing nets; to say nothing of snatch hooks on the end of a pole. It is not to be wondered at considering the long and exhausting time they take over spawning, that they should be in the very worst possible condition for several weeks after that operation; they are long, thin, slimy, and even unwholesome as food, and should not on any account be tried for before August, in fact, I don't consider them in condition before the first of October. If my opinion was asked as to what I should consider to be a proper close time for jack, I should most certainly say, between the first day of February, and the first day of September.

Pike, under favourable circumstances, will grow to a very large size, but their well being depends upon the locality and condition of the water they inhabit. Deep holes and weedy shallows should both be in evidence, while if the place is a lake with a gravelly bottom, a stream of some sort should run right through it, so that a constant supply of fresh water could be assured, and last, but not least, the lake should also contain an abundance of natural food; these conditions together with a careful preservation, would be condusive to these fish reaching their very heaviest weight. As to what that weight is likely to be, it is difficult to determine, for so many fables and romances have been written on the subject; that we have to be very careful before accepting all of them. We are told that in some of the large

Irish lakes they have been taken of the extraordinary weight of eighty pounds, but I don't suppose anyone ever saw one that weight, it was most probably a tradition handed down from father to son, and most likely grew in the process. If tremendous pike like those were got by our fathers in the days that are past, how is it that with our improved tackle and means of getting at them, we never hear of anything approaching that weight being captured. Pliny, the ancient writer, mentions a fish which he called the Esox, and which attained the weight of a 1,000lbs; but it cannot be identified with the Esox of the present day. I should say the very top weight would not exceed forty to forty-five pounds. We have authentic instances of late years of odd ones nearly reaching the former weight; but they were like angels' visits, few and far between. Perhaps the heaviest brace of pike that have ever been taken by any one angler, with rod and line, were the pair taken by Mr. Jardine, which were weighed in at a Club, and registered no less than thirty-six pounds each on the average. We hear of odd ones being taken every season in Ireland, that reach thirty pounds; and sometimes, perhaps once in every two or three seasons, one will reach thirty-four, or thirty-five pounds. An article appeared in the "Angler," last December, 1896, giving an account of an extraordinary female pike, that had been taken dead from Dowdeswell reservoir, near Cheltenham, which reached the weight of sixty pounds; at least it was said to have weighed that, but one gentleman who saw the fish, said he should be inclined to knock at least 10lbs off. It appears that the weighing in had been done in a very hasty manner, owing to the fact that decomposition had set in; and the smell was something alarming. So I am afraid this pike can only be set down among the list of guess-weights, and cannot be accepted by any means. It was also said that the Duke of Newcastle has a pike, which he himself or one of his family caught in Clumber Lake (a large sheet of water close to his Grace's Nottinghamshire seat), which weighed, when captured, 42 ½ lbs.; but the Duke contradicted this and said, if my memory is correct, that gossip this time had added eight pounds to its original weight. Clumber Lake, I should say, is one of the finest pike preserves in England; and if

large pike can be found anywhere, surely that is the place
to look for them. I once asked old Charlie Hudson, a
Trent professional fisherman, who had fished a celebrated
reach of that river for nigh on fifty years, if he or any of his
patrons had taken many pike over twenty pounds in weight
from those splendid waters. Four only was his answer;
and during the long period referred to, he had some hundreds of patrons and customers; the united weight of the
four was 87½lbs., largest a trifle over 25lbs., and the
strangest part about the capture of the latter, was that it was
taken with a worm, when bream fishing in that tremendously
deep hole on the Lower Trent known as Dunham Dubs.
Taking the Trent all round it is only occasionally that speci-
mens exceeding twenty pounds are taken. The Hampshire
Avon, perhaps, is as good as any other river in England for
large jack, some odd times we hear of one being taken that
scaled up to nearly thirty pounds. The angler can well be
satisfied as things go nowadays, if he can get one from any
public waters that will go from twenty to twenty-five pounds,
and this, perhaps, will only be once in a lifetime, while if he
gets a dozen fish during the whole of his angling career, that
would go from twelve to eighteen pounds apiece, why he
may consider himself fortunate, unless he has access to real
good private waters.

I once heard a very old and observant angler naturalist
say, that he firmly believed two kinds of pike existed in
British waters; externally there was little or nothing to tell
the difference, except the size, one sort he believed would
reach 20 or 30lb., the other never exceeded four pounds,
and in support of this he cited the case of two sheets of
water, some miles apart, exactly similar in their size, depth,
and general characteristics, both had gravelly bottoms, both
were fringed with weeds, flags, and rushes; both were fed
by small streams from the higher lands, each contained a
good supply of eels, tench, roach, bream, and perch; in
fact, the general surroundings of the two were as far as
could be ascertained, exactly similar. He had fished in both
of them for many years—in one he had taken pike up to
20lb. In the other he never saw, nor yet caught one that
exceeded 4lb. There may be something in this; but sev-

eral other things may also have to be taken into account before a true decision can be arrived at on that point. Shortly then, as this seems to be a question that a lot of interest is evinced in, we may say that a forty pounder is a tip-topper, and one not likely to be caught above once in twenty years, whereas if a lucky fisherman did manage to fairly and squarely land, with rod and line, a brace of pike that exceeds Mr. Jardine's pair in size, why, all I can say is, that not only should the fish be carefully set up, but the angler as well, and he ought to, at the very least, have a niche all to himself in Westminster Abbey, with a brass plate setting forth his achievement. Some anglers seem to think that jack and pike are two separate and distinct fish; that there is a distinction if not much difference between them. Years ago it was an accepted rule to call this fish, if under four or five pounds in weight, a jack, and anything over the latter weight a pike, but gradually this distinctive title has been given up, and all of them, no matter how large or how small, have of late years been more often called jack than pike; so the reader must bear in mind that in using the two names in the following pages, I refer to one and the same fish. We are told by the learned in such matters that a jack will reach eight inches in length during his first year, after hatching from the ova; that during his second year he will go up to fifteen inches; and in his third, total up to twenty, or possibly he might scale as much as four pounds when three years old. After this he increases at the rate of from two or three pounds a year until he is twelve years old; after which he decreases slightly and gets still more thin every year, as old age creeps on him. Naturalists have given him a lease of life extending to forty years, and say that he is the longest lived of any of our fresh water fish; and that when one is captured in the last stages of consumption, long, lanky, and thin, it is a very old fish. I remember a friend of mine once capturing a jack in the Ouse, some three of four miles below Huntingdon, that was the most extraordinary I ever saw; it was no less than 38 inches in length, it had a tremendous head and mouth, and yet it scaled only 6¾lb. I never saw such an eel-like body attached to a pike before; its teeth were wonderfully long, as

black as ink, and quite soft. I should say that those calcu-
lations as to the weight a jack will put on in a given number
of years will depend a good deal on the nature and character
of the water he inhabits. I believe it would have to be an
extra good water for a jack in a natural way to reach four
pounds when three years old, and then increase to seven
pounds in his next year. If he is an inhabitant of an in-
different pond, where he only could get an occasional
frog, a young moor hen, or a mouthful of tadpoles, it would
probably take him ten years to put on four pounds.

As I said at the outset of this chapter, the pike is a fish
that is very much sought after by the angler, and good pike
fishing, out of public waters at any rate, can hardly now-a-
days be expected. When I say good fishing, I mean as it was
even during my memory, where a dozen good fish to one rod
in a day's spinning was thought nothing extra. Or go back
a little further still; but for all that during the memory of
an old angler still living, who told me last time I saw him,
that he could remember the time when flags and rushes
grew in abundance all along the brink of the Trent, and had
seen the big jack bolt out of the reeds every few steps; and
when employed as puntsman by the late Dr. Waterworth
and Mr. Cafferata, he could remember them taking as many
as thirty pike during a single afternoon, many of them fish
from eight to fifteen pounds apiece. It was also nothing
unusual for Tom Beck (an old netter still living), to go down
the river to the Meering ferry and Sutton Holme in those
days, and take in a net a hundredweight of good jack during
a single evening. I can myself remember very well, the
late Sam Hibbert, when he rented the Staythorpe fishery on
the Trent, getting some splendid bags of pike, nearly every-
time he cared to go. But since those days pike fishermen
have increased a hundred-fold, and any public water known
to contain jack is nearly hunted to death, with the result that
they are wofully thinned down; and it is only occasionally
that a good bag is made. Suitable pike waters should be
constantly re-stocked now-a-days, and a stringent bye-law
should be made and enforced, to regulate the size of jack
allowed to be taken. All this means money, but still I
firmly believe that angling and preservation societies will

have to tackle the subject if decent jack fishing in public
waters is to be enjoyed much longer. Far different, however, is a day in a real good private water; if everything
is favourable the sport to be had would be something to
be remembered. There are still, however, a few very fair
public pike waters in England, the vast army of fishermen
notwithstanding. The rivers and broads of Norfolk and
Suffolk being notable examples. The Ouse, as it flows from
Buckinghamshire right away down to Denver Sluice, being
very fair indeed in many of its reaches; while the County of
Lincoln still upholds its reputation for jack. The best
season's pike fishing I ever enjoyed, taking it all through,
was had less than ten years ago, when I lived on the banks
of the Ouse. During that season I took in public water,
with rod and line, during my spare time, which was generally
two half-days a week—weather and water permitting—109
sizeable jack, not counting the scores put back that were
undersized. The most I ever landed from that river in one
day was 21, but only seven of them went over 4lbs. The
great bulk of my fish have been taken spinning. On two occasions at least, I can remember having had more and far
heavier jack than the instance just referred to; but they
were from a private water, and a good many years ago. I
just mention this as fishermen, in general, like to know how
a writer himself has got on; but I may have to refer to this
again, when dealing with the various subjects in the chapters
that follow. The anxious novice who would like to become
a successful pike fisherman, must make up his mind, if he
follows this branch of angling in public waters, to two things,
viz., he is bound to catch more fish under four pounds than
over that weight, and if he gets three or four jack during a
day's spinning or live-baiting, he can consider himself extremely lucky. I should say that pike fishing engaged the
attention of our forefathers a good many years ago, and trolling with a dead gorge bait, and live baiting, more or less
after the fashion that we do it now, were the methods most
in vogue. Dame Juliana Berners, who wrote the very first
book on angling that was ever penned, gives some very
queer and amusing instructions in the art of catching pike.
I give one or two examples, as they may prove interesting to

those fishermen who never have a chance of seeing the good old lady's book : —

"Take a codlynge hoke, and take a roche or a fresh heeryng, and a wyre with an hole in the ende, and put it in at the mouth, and out at the taylle, down by the ridge of the fresshe herryng; and thenne put the hoke in after, and drawe the hoke into the cheke of the freshe heeryng; then put a plumbe of lead upon your lyne a yarde longe from your hoke, and a flote in mid waye betwene; and caste it in a pytte where the pyke usyth, and this is the best and moost surest crafte of takynge the pyke. Another manere of takynge him there is; take a frosshe (frog) and put it on your hoke, at the necke, betwene the skynne and the body, on the backe half, and put on a flote a yerde therefro, and caste it where the pyke hauntyth, and ye shall have hym. Another manere: take the same bayte, and put it in assafetida, and caste it in the water wyth a corde and a corke, and ye shall not fayl of hym." And then again the good Dame instructeth: —"And if ye lyst to have a good sporte, thenne tye the corde to a gose fote, and ye shall have a gode halyngne, whether the gose or the pyke shall have the better."

This sort of sport, tying a baited hook to the leg of a goose, seems to have been highly popular in former times; for another old writer on fishing matters tells us that : —

"The principle sport to take a pike is to take a goose or gander, or duck; take one of the pike lines, tie the line under the left wing, and over the right wing, about the body, as a man weareth his belt; turn the goose off into the pond where the pikes are; there is no doubt of sport, with great pleasure, betwixt the goose and the pike; it is the greatest sport and pleasure that a noble gentleman in Shropshire doth give his friends entertainment with."

Another account of a struggle between a pike and a gander, was published many years ago, and ran as follows: —"A farmer in the immediate neighbourhood of Lochmaben, Dumfriesshire, kept a gander, who not only had a great trick of wandering himself, but also delighted in piloting forth his cackling harem to weary themselves in circumnavigating their native lake, or in straying amid forbidden

fields on the opposite shore. Wishing to check this vagrant
habit, he one day seized the gander as he was about to
spring into the pure breast of his native element, and, tying
a large fish hook to his leg, to which was attached part of
a dead frog, he suffered him to proceed upon his voyage of
discovery. As had been anticipated, this bait soon caught
the eye of a greedy pike, which, swallowing the deadly hook,
not only arrested the progress of the astonished gander, but
forced him to perform half-a-dozen somersaults on the face
of the water! For some time the struggle was most amusing, the fish pulling and the bird screaming with all its
might, the one attempting to fly and the other attempting to
swim from the invisible enemy; the gander the one moment
losing, and the next regaining his centre of gravity, and
casting between whiles many a rueful look at his snow white
fleet of geese and goslings, who cackled out their sympathy
for their afflicted commodore. At length victory declared
in favour of the feathered angler, who, bearing away for the
nearest shore, landed on the smooth green grass one of the
finest pike ever caught in the castle loch. This adventure
is said to have cured the gander of his propensity for
wandering."

This pike fishing by tying the bait to the leg of a goose
smacks very much of trimmer fishing with a moveable trimmer all alive and kicking. I should not suppose that any-
body would attempt to entertain their friends with sport of
this description, now-a-days, whatever might have been
thought about it fifty years ago. As far back as the reign of
Henry II., the pike formed part of the coat of arms of the
Lucy, or Lucie family, and is one of the earliest recorded
instances of fish being used in English heraldry. Old His-
torians tell us, "that during the reign of Edward I. this fish
was so very scarce and dear, that very few could afford to
eat it, the price being double that of salmon, and ten times
higher than either turbot or cod." A well known authority
says that the reason of this is most likely in the fact, that
pike had then only just been introduced into this country,
and as a natural consequence was very scarce. Coming
down a little later to the time of Edward III. we find, " that
this fish was most carefully preserved, kept in stews, and

c

fed.   In 1446 jack was one of the chief dishes in the High
Church festival given in that year by George Neville, Arch-
bishop of York.   During the reign of Henry VIII. it
fetched as much again as house lamb in February, and a
very small pickerel was dearer than a fat capon; and jack
figured on all the menus of civic banquets in London and
elsewhere for many generations."   Personally I look upon
pike as being a very fair fish for the table, that is, if the
water they were caught in was of first class quality; if he
came out of a muddy stagnant pond, I don't suppose he
would be up to much; but a good river or lake pike, where
the water is fresh, the bottom gravelly, and the food plentiful, is by no means to be despised.   I quoted just now some
examples from old history, in which this fish was very highly
esteemed.   An old couplet ran thus:
            " Lo ! the rich pike, to entertain your guest,
            Smokes on the board, and decks a royal feast."
While on the other hand some of the ancients did not think
much of him, for Ausonius, the Latin poet, writing about
the fourth century of the Christian era, says of him as
            " Unknown at friendship's hospitable board,
            Smokes 'midst the smoky tavern's coarsest food."
Small pike, of say three to four pounds, are the best if
cleaned as soon after capture as possible, well washed and
dried, and then split open like filletting.   Remove the backbone, also cut off the head, tail and fins, and then divide
each half in two; fry crisp and clean over a clear fire in a
frying pan, with a good lump, say five or six ounces of fresh,
pure lard; turn each piece over as soon as sufficiently cooked
on the under side, sprinkle with a little egg and bread
crumbs and serve smoking hot (it is the best for the lard to
be at boiling point before dropping in the fish).   If the pike
runs somewhat larger, say from five to nine pounds, it is the
best plan to put a couple of good handfulls of salt into its
mouth, and hang it up in a cool place, tail downwards, for
five or six hours, or possibly longer if the fish is larger; it
can then be cleaned, washed, and prepared in the usual
manner, and either steamed or boiled, the same as cod, and
served with parsley sauce.   Be sure it is well cooked—until
the flesh will flake nicely away from the bones, and if the

fish was in good condition it will be firm, white, and tooth-some. On no account cook a pike from a muddy, stagnant pond, nor yet one from anywhere before the month of September, or you are likely to get a wrong impression as to what one of these fish is like. They are in the very worst possible condition during the summer—thin, flabby, and unwholesome.

Just a word or two now as to the various methods of tak-ing the pike in a legitimate manner. First, by spinning with an arrangement of hooks fixed in a dead bait, in such a manner that when this bait is thrown across the water and drawn back again it looks like a thing of life. Second, by spinning with an artificial, worked exactly the same as just described for a dead bait. Third, by working a dead gorge tackle in places where it is impossible for weeds and obstruc-tions to try either spinning or live-baiting. These three plans are worked with a similar leaded trace for each, and no floats. Fourth, by one or two floats and a live bait fixed on snap tackle, so that the pike can be hooked directly he attacks the bait. Fifth, by float tackle similar to the one just named, except the hook is a live gorge one, which has to be swallowed by the pike before he can be hooked. Sixth, by paternostering with one or more live baits, a lead, and no float. Seventh, by legering with a live bait sunk to the bottom of deep water with the aid of a heavy bored bullet, a live gorge tackle or a semi-snap gorge being used and no float. There are several other methods of taking pike, such as liggering, trimmering, trailing, etc., etc.,; but these are not sportsmanlike methods, and should be care-fully avoided, unless the jack are far too numerous in a private water, and the proprietor wants to thin them down. The seven plans given above, of course varying the process to suit certain localities, are about all I dare mention to be within the bounds of legitimate pike fishing. I will try in the following chapters to fully and carefully explain the whole of them.

CHAPTER II.

THE PIKE *(continued).*

PIKE RODS, REELS, AND LINES.

The pike rod—What it has to do—How it should be made—Different woods and canes suitable for pike rods—Rod rings and ferrules—Pike reels—The Malloch casting reel—Slater's cage guard reel—Allcock's pike reels—The plain Nottingham reel—The line—How to dress or waterproof a pike line—The line dryer—Landing nets and gaff hooks—Flight cases and haversacks—Rod and tackle varnish.

There seems to be a tendency among rod makers in general nowadays to sacrifice strength in a rod for the sake of extra lightness and elegance, and in no rod is this more apparent than in what they are pleased to call pike rods. Even pike fishermen themselves are smitten with the same sort of mania, and will insist in having a rod for jack fishing that is totally inadequate for the work they now and again call on it to do.   Personally I am far from being a believer in a heavy, clumsy weapon for the sport now under notice; but I like to draw the line at something like reason, and start with, at any rate, a rod that is not likely to play me false at a critical moment.   I have seen jack rods in use that hardly looked stout enough for fly fishing for chub, and as for throwing a bait with any degree of accuracy, why, that seemed out of the question altogether.   I once saw an angler using a fourteen-foot grilse rod for spinning for pike, and I think I never saw anything more erratic in my life, the bait very often landing wide on the grassy bank on which he stood, instead of sailing gracefully and gently into midstream.   I found, on trying myself, that the fault lay more in the rod than the fisherman, and if he had discarded the top altogether and had an end ring fitted on the second joint, he would have got on a lot better.   "But," says one of these believers in extra light and flimsy rods, " I once killed a six-pound barbel and a four-pound trout on that rod ; and if it will kill fish like those, why it surely ought to be good enough to kill any jack I am likely to get hold of." True, my friend, I should have to reply to this argument, because I don't look upon a jack as being anything like such a good fighter as a barbel, while he is also any number of degrees behind a good trout. But this is not altogether it ; if the rod had nothing else to do except kill the pike when hooked, why, I should have nothing further to say in the matter, because the actual killing of the fish, especially in clear and unobstructed water, is one of the easiest jobs the rod is called upon to perform.

When the angler selects a rod for pike fishing, he must bear in mind the following three things : —First, some considerable strain is required in casting out a heavy bait ; second, when a good jack is hooked and in full sail for his favourite weed bed or old root, it wants a fairly powerful rod to turn him ; third, when you get hung up in some tough old weeds with a strong line and gimp tackle, very considerable force sometimes has to be used to loosen it. These three points are of frequent occurrence in pike fishing, especially in weedy rivers, lakes, and backwaters, so that a very light, flimsy rod would soon get broken, or else strained beyond recovery. I don't recommend a hop pole or anything like that, but a rod fairly stiff and powerful, with a nice spring in the top, sufficient to cast out the bait comfortably and accurately.

Pike rods are made nowadays of a variety of materials, and in a variety of patterns ; some of them, I am bound to say, more for ornament than use. Hickory, greenheart, lancewood, ash, two or three different kinds of cane, and even split and built-up cane, with steel centres, all coming more or less into requisition ; but as the latter are extremely expensive weapons, they are utterly out of the question as far as working men anglers are concerned. Some men will swear by a rod made entirely of greenheart, and certainly this wood, when of first-class quality, is very good indeed ; but in my opinion, based on many years' experience at the rod-maker's bench, it is not exactly an unqualified success, the chief objection being the very great weight of this wood, coupled with a tendency to snap short off, sometimes without any apparent reason, and no flaw discoverable in the grain of the wood. Of course I am aware that some lovely rods are built from greenheart, that have stood any amount of hard work for years, and to counteract the weight some of them are built up with a cork grip, which certainly does reduce the weight somewhat. A pike rod built with an ash butt and lancewood centre and top is a very fair weapon indeed, but the same objection can be raised against this, as against an all-greenheart one—viz., extra weight in using. Then again there are pike rods made of what some people call whole cane; but this in eight cases out of every ten is not whole cane at all, but simply the very cheapest that a rod maker can buy—viz., "Tonquin." Now, this cane tapers very little, the joints of the rod are nearly as thick at one end as they are at the other, and consequently there is not the power in the lower joints that I like to see in a pike rod. The cane that seems to me to be the very best that can be employed in making a pike rod is what is known as East India cane, and when it is mottled and spotted in an attractive manner, why, I don't know a handsomer or more useful weapon. This material of late years has sprung to the front in an amazing manner, and certainly when we look at it, it is admirably adapted for the purpose, for the rods made from it are light, stiff, and very powerful—three attributes of the very first importance—and when all three are combined in one, why, the value is very much increased. This cane is tapered more than any other I know; a piece four feet long sometimes is as much as one and a half inches in diameter at one end, and only three-quarters of an inch at the other. As good and as cheap a pike rod for all practical purposes that can be used, and one that will be within the reach of any working man angler, should be made of this cane, and in three lengths, or not more than four at the very outside, personally I prefer three—viz., butt and one or two centre joints of East India male cane, and one or two tops, according to fancy, of good tough lancewood or greenheart, the former for choice, as I fancy lancewood has more spring than greenheart; the latter seems to be so very stiff, and does not play as I like to see a rod top play. Greenheart tops have more resistance than lancewood, I am aware, but still I have tried both, and the balance of my opinion goes in favour of lancewood. Twelve feet is a good useful length for a pike rod, particularly for live-baiting or paternostering, while eleven feet would be much nicer and easier for spinning, and as the top of a live-baiting rod should be a trifle more springy than the top of a spinning rod, I recommend two tops for the various purposes, one the full length of the other joints, and tapered nicely to the point for paternostering or live-baiting, and the other nine or ten inches shorter, and a shade stiffer for spinning. The ferrule on the butt of a three-joint rod of this description should not be less on any account than three-quarters of an inch, while it would be all the better if it went nearly seven-eighths of an inch, inside diameter; while the one on the centre joint should not be smaller than from seven-sixteenths to half-an-inch, measuring the diameter inside the ferrule; and I might add that these ferrules should grip the cane properly, and be fixed over the outside; the cane itself should not on any account be cut away to receive the ferrule. Of course it is better to have brazings at each end of the joint, and also a dowel or tenon that fits the hole inside the cane fairly and well, and this tenon that projects beyond the brass counter at bottom of the joints can also be brazed if the angler likes, as it would be less liable to stick tight in when wet. This matter of fitting the joints of a pike rod with properly fitting ferrules and tenons is of more importance than some amateurs would think, because if these joints did not fit tight and close up, the strain of constantly throwing would bend the ferrule out of its proper shape, and the rod look like a dog's hind leg. I should say that the average weight of a weapon of this class would go something like 22 oz. It is difficult to lay down a hard and fast rule, as the cane varies somewhat; some rods might run up to 25 oz., while a similar one, as far as outside measurements were concerned, would only total up to 19 or 20 oz. The rings also should be a matter of consideration, and they should be fixed on the rod in such a manner and be of such a size that the line, no matter in what manner or style the bait is thrown, should run freely through them without the possibility of a catch or tangle; and, for instance, if the angler throws the bait with the line coiled at his feet, and there happens to be a snarl in it, when a pike runs with the bait the rings should be such that the line, kink and all, will easily slip through, instead of being brought up with a jerk by jamming tight in the ring. I don't like the "Bell's Life" rings on a trolling rod; they don't stand the wear and tear of throwing with a stout line and a heavy bait. These rings are splendid for the lighter work of chubbing down a stream; but in pike fishing, especially spinning, I found them to be a mistake. In the first place this ring is of a tolerable length, and the binding that fastens them to the rod is fixed at each end; the centre of the ring is not firmly bound to the rod, and the consequence is that a sudden jerk or strong drag with the line pulls one end of the ring away from its bindings, especially if those bindings are somewhat old and worn, and would be likely to cause unpleasantness; and in the second place these rings are made of rather soft metal, which the line soon cuts and grooves. If these rings could be made in hardened steel they would be a decided improvement on the old-fashioned ones. Taking rings for a pike rod all round, I fancy there are none to beat the snake pattern, made of rust-proof bronzed and hardened steel; and in fixing them on the rod they should be graduated, that is, the largest on the butt and the smallest near the top end; and this small ring should not be any less than will comfortably allow a medium sized lead pencil, say three-eighths or seven-sixteenths of an inch in diameter, to pass through. The ring on the butt can be about five-eighths of an inch in size, and this in a three-piece rod should be fixed immediately under the ferrule. I have seen rings fixed on the butt within a foot or 14 inches from the reel; but this, if we look at it carefully, will be found another mistake, because in using the fair sized reel that is necessary in pike fishing, when the ring is so near it, the line when threaded through forms too acute an angle, and grinds and cuts it more than is good for the lasting qualities of the very best line that ever was plaited. When the ring is higher up the butt, this angle is nothing like so apparent, and the friction on the line a good deal less. If the angler will consider a moment he will find there is more in this than mere theory, for I have seen good pike lines utterly ruined in a very short time by grinding in a butt ring fixed in close proximity to the reel. Shortly, then, we will say there should be one ring on the butt of a pike rod as near the ferrule as possible, three rings on the centre joint, and four without counting the end ring on the top, and the nearer to the tip the closer to each other should these rings be. The end ring of all will be all the better if it has also an inner ring of hardened steel or phosphor bronze fitted in it in such a manner that it will revolve or twist round and round. This will also help to preserve the line, as naturally there is considerable wear and friction going on at the extreme end, of a spinning rod especially.

The winch fittings should be about eight inches from the end of the butt, and these can either be the plain old-fashioned three-ring fittings, or the newer Universal or gradu-ated ones, whichever the fisherman likes, the latter perhaps being slightly the best, as they are so constructed that they will securely hold any size of reel without any of the cane being cut away to form the slot or bed.

The end of the rod can be finished off with either a brass cap, a hard-wood knob, or an indiarubber button, according to fancy. I like my pike rod to play well in the top—that is, dressed down nice and tapering from the ferrule—because I have found by a lengthy experience in casting that the throw is cleaner, easier, and more accurate if the rod feels stiff and powerful in the lower end of it, and a kind of switch at the tip end.

There is just one more point I should like to say a few words on, and that it, some anglers recommend this pike rod to have a hollow butt, on purpose to hold the spare top that is not then in use; but my advice is—don't, decidedly; be-cause if you notice there are knots or joints at intervals down this cane that gives it its strength and rigidity. If these are cut away by being bored out, the butt is likely to splinter up and crack after being in use some little time. And then again a pike rod top, with its fair sized rings and top ring would want a butt of more than ordinary thickness to comfortably carry it.

A good rod, such as I have attempted to describe, would
run up to fifteen or sixteen shillings, or possibly a shilling
or two more, if everything was of the very best quality. A
very fair weapon that would be extremely useful to the working man pike angler who only gets out occasionally could be

FIG. 1. A CHEAP PIKE ROD.

produced from eight to ten shillings. Fig. 1 shows an extremely useful jack rod that is built in four lengths for convenience of carriage if the longer-jointed one would be too
awkward to carry about. The material of this is East India
cane and lancewood tops. Fig. 2 is an exact reproduction
of my own pike rod. This, too, is built of East India cane,
and its fittings and rings are similar to what I have described
in the foregoing pages. I have touched upon this question
of a pike rod in a rather lengthy manner, and some may say
gone rather unnecessarily into certain details; but I was
anxious to give the would-be pike fisherman a few hints as
to what he really required, so as to save him trouble and expense afterwards. When he goes to his rod maker now, he
will be in a position to tell him exactly what he wants, and

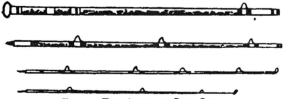

FIG. 2. THE AUTHOR'S PIKE ROD.

the results are likely to be more satisfactory on both sides.
I must let this be my excuse, to say nothing of the fact that
in the very few pages that I have devoted to this special subject of rods there is the experience of nearly a lifetime at
the rod maker's bench and the riverside recorded. One
more little thing that I had nearly forgotten in connection

with this subject, and it is very nearly the most important of
all. Many times I am asked the question as to whether a
very stiff top added to a light chub or barbel rod would not
make that rod for all practical purposes a good strong pike
rod? I am bound to answer all such with a very decided
" no." Strange as it may seem, it is nevertheless true that
the stronger and stiffer the top is in a light rod, the weaker
does that rod become. The old saying that " a chain is no
stronger than its weakest link " can be applied with even
more force to rods. They are no stronger than their weakest
points, and instead of a strong stiff top making the rod
stronger in itself, it is very often a source of weakness. More
strain would be thrown on the second joint, and eventually,
if the rod was kept at this heavy work, that joint, at any
rate, would be utterly ruined. I am strongly in favour of
having a pike rod made for that special purpose, and use it
for pike fishing alone. I am not very much in love with
combination rods, although they can be constructed with a
very fair amount of success, but they have to be specially
built. What I want just now to impress on the mind of the
would-be pike fisherman is this : if he has an old favourite
roach or chub rod, he must not be deluded into having an
extra strong and stiff top fitted to it, under the impression
that it is going to make a strong pike rod, or he will probably regret it when too late.

A reel is a necessary article in a pike fisherman's outfit,
because he cannot very well fish for jack with a tight line
tied halfway down his rod, the same as some roach fishermen do, he must have a pretty fair length of line, and a reel
is necessary for one thing to hold it. Pike reels are made
at the present time in a variety of patterns, and at nearly
all prices ; but I consider a good stout Nottingham wood
reel as good as anything that can be tried. It is not so absolutely necessary to have an easy-going centre-pin reel for
this work, as it is in chub fishing down a stream. A centre-
pin is almost too lively for a jack reel. It ought, however,
to run fairly free, and as I always in spinning cast my bait
directly from the reel, and look upon this method as being
the very best to adopt, perhaps I may be excused if my particular fancy turns to these wooden reels. A four-and-a-half-

inch one is the best size; it should not be less than four inches, at any rate, and it ought to be made of good dry and hard walnut, of pretty substantial build, and be fitted with a strong brass cross-back. A moveable check action is also a very useful addition to these reels, as it can then be used for all purposes and all styles of pike fishing. A good plain

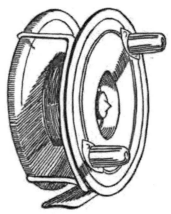

FIG. 3. PLAIN PIKE REEL, WITH LINE GUARD.

spindle reel is my particular fancy. I don't strongly recommend a centre-pin, although scores of good pike fishermen use them. A pike reel such as I have described would run from six to eight shillings. A working man need not spend any more than that, as he would not find one of the most elaborately got-up and expensive reels one little bit better for all practical purposes. Some anglers say that they cannot, try as they will, cast a bait direct from the reel in what we call the Nottingham style. They either have to coil the line at their feet, or else use one or other of the wonderfully constructed reels that are supposed to be helps to this style. It is not a very successful plan to coil the line at the feet, because there are places where the angler has to stand knee-deep among flags, reeds, thistles, thorns, and all sorts of rank undergrowth, where the line would catch and be generally aggravating. One of the best-known of these casting

reels was invented by Mr. P. D. Mallock, of Perth, and bears
his name.   When a bait is cast by this reel the barrel or revolving portion of it does not turn round ; it is fitted up with
a contrivance, or a sort of a hinge, so that the portion of the
reel that holds the line can be turned or twisted half round.
When the cast is made the line is pulled from the drum or
barrel a good deal like pulling thread from the end of a
bobbin or spool, the force of the cast causing the line to unwind itself as the bait travels to its destination.   As soon as
the bait strikes the water, of course, the line stops, and the
revolving or drum part of the reel has to be turned back
again into its original position before the line and bait can
be worked or spun home again.   When the bait is thrown
with this reel there are no handles spinning round to rap the
incautious novice over the fingers, and no revolving plates
into which the line can suddenly catch and jam itself tight.
The reel only revolves when the angler wishes to spin his
bait and recover the line that he has thrown out, or when
a fish bolts off with the bait.   There seems to me to be two
or three objections to this reel, the greatest of which would
be the extreme difficulty an angler would experience in spinning his bait over very shallow and weedy places, which
situations, I might add, are very often the best places in
which to find pike.   Sometimes it is necessary to begin
spinning or working the bait home again after a cast the very
moment the bait strikes the water.   If it is allowed to sink
even six inches under the surface the hooks would catch
among the weeds, and the cast be spoiled.   It seems to me
that the time that must elapse between the bait getting to its
destination and turning the revolving portion of the reel back
into its original position before that bait can be wound back
again would be fatal to its success in very shallow and weedy
water.   In very deep and unobstructed lakes and rivers, of
course, this objection does not count, there would be plenty
of time to manipulate the reel before the bait reached the
bottom or anywhere near it.   Another point against this reel
is by being made of metal it is rather heavy, and would be
tiring to spin with all day ; and they are also very expensive,
a good one running to something like thirty shillings.   There
are, however, scores and scores of good pike fishermen in

Ireland and Scotland who swear by them. They say that
they cannot for the life of them throw a bait direct from a
Nottingham reel, and find the Malloch one of the most useful inventions they ever tried. Personally, I never used one
in actual pike fishing; I have seen and examined them.
Once I tried my hand at throwing a bait across a grass lawn
with one, and consider them wonderfully ingenious, and calculated to assist those pike fishermen who are really baffled
in their efforts to master the peculiarities of the ordinary
Nottingham reel. Another pike reel that has been a great
favourite for many years now was invented by Mr. David
Slater, and christened by him " The Combination." In an
ordinary Nottingham reel, anglers who are not very expert
pike bait throwers find that the line in casting gets outside
and hanks itself round the handles, or even sometimes a
long loop drops down and catches round the bottom of the
butt end of the rod. The revolving barrel of Slater's reel
runs in a cage that is fixed firmly to the back, and certainly
this is the best invention that I am as yet acquainted with
for keeping the line in its proper position. The Bickerdyke
line guard is also supposed, when fixed to an ordinary Nottingham reel, to stop the line from overrunning; but this
guard, useful as it undoubtedly is, is not, in my opinion,
equal to Slater's cage guard. In the Bickerdyke guard there
is nothing to prevent loose line from falling out at the under
side of the reel. It does, however, keep the line from falling over the top and catching round the handles. I have
had one of Slater's cage guard reels in constant use for
many years now for pike fishing. I believe my reel was the
first, or very nearly the first, that Mr. Slater made; anyhow
I have had it since 1882. It is a plain spindle reel without
check action, four and a half inches in diameter. Those
anglers who really must spin with the line coiled at their
feet, and really cannot be persuaded to try any other plan,
need not be so particular as to the choice of a reel, a plain
wooden or brass one, provided it is large enough to hold
the line, will do very well.

Of late years so many reels have been invented for pike
fishing that the anxious novice is apt to get bewildered, and
be nearly at his wits end in making a selection. There is

the "Coxon," that runs round at nearly a breath of wind; but I don't think this really was invented as a pike reel, although I make no doubt it could be used as one on a pinch. It is much more valuable as a stream-fishing reel for roach and chub. Then there is another with an aluminium drum, so carefully and accurately running upon a steel centre that the very lightest minnow can be cast direct with it. This reel is called the "Duplex," and where it differs from the ordinary Nottingham wooden reel is the fact that while the bait is travelling to its destination after being thrown, the handle does not spin round and round; and here it also differs from the "Mallock," mentioned some time ago. The latter has to be twisted half round before the bait can be wound home again. With the "Duplex" the line can be recovered and wound back again in an instant. The "Duplex" reel is manufactured by Messrs. S. Allcock and Co., of Redditch, which fact is generally admitted by expert anglers of the present day to be a sufficient guarantee that the quality is beyond reproach. Of course these reels are rather expensive, and hardly to be thought about by the ordinary working men anglers; but these men need not despair and think that they cannot cast out a pike bait properly unless they have one or the other of them to assist in the operation. I think I shall be able to give such a few instructions in the following pages that, coupled with a little practise, will enable them to cast out a bait clean and neat without tangle or catch with only a plain spindle Nottingham reel, costing at most a few shillings to do it with. I can call to mind some of the very best working men pike fishermen who ever threw a bait across river, lake, or stream, who never used any other reel than a plain, easy-going Nottingham. The whole secret of casting out a spinning bait direct from the reel without overrunning, jerking the bait off the hooks by a sudden stoppage of the line when in mid air, or having a beautiful tangle of line on the barrel of the reel when the bait reaches its destination, or having the fingers rapped by the revolving handles, lies in a judicious selection of the rod, reel, and line, coupled with the easy forward swing that alone is necessary to get the bait out to nearly any distance, and above all to the proper and well-timed

pressure of the finger on the revolving edge of the reel.
First, the rod should be so constructed that it will play well
at the tip end, and be stiff and strong at its lower joints.
Some makers and anglers may tell you that it is impossible
to cast out a pike bait properly unless you have a very
springy rod—one that will bend round, nearly like a fly rod,
from the tip down to the handle; but my experience is that
the top itself should bend well, the second joint bend a little
towards the thin end of it, while the butt and part of the
second joint should be stiff and rigid in the hand.   The
distance and accuracy of the cast is very much improved by
having the rod as near to the above requirements as possible.
Secondly, the reel itself should run very smoothly; it should
not wobble at all, nor yet " chatter," as we call it, while the
bait is travelling to its destination.   The back, or fixed part,
and the barrel or revolving part should fit close together, so
that there is no play or looseness between the nut on end of
the spindle, and the brass plate under it.   There is more in
this than meets the eye of the casual observer, because if
the reel chatters and does not run smoothly and well, more
force is required in the cast to start the bait upon its journey.   When the young pike fisherman selects this article of
his outfit, he should carefully take stock of it, see that it is
strong and well made, that it has a stout brass cross-back,
is fitted up with a good moveable check action, and that the
handles on the front are fitted to strong oval plates, screwed
firmly to the wood by a screw at each end.   These oval
plates are a great protection to the handles, as without them,
in the constant winding that a pike spinning reel is sub-
jected to, they are liable to work loose.

Having satisfied himself on the above points, the novice
should then hold the reel firmly by the back in his left
hand, and with his right tap the edge of the revolving part
smartly downwards.   If it will revolve freely and smoothly
without wobble or shake, and feels firm and rigid under the
brass nut, and its spindle is not loose and shaky, he has
without doubt got a reel that is admirably adapted for throwing out and working home a pike bait in this most deadly
and easy style; and I might add that he should not on any
consideration give more than eight shillings for it.

Thirdly, the spinning line should also be selected with a good deal of care. A strong, heavy, waterproof line is not a success by any means when used as a casting line direct from the reel. It should be an undressed silk, or at most only very slightly and smoothly dressed, and the size need not be too thick, nor must it on the other hand be too thin. I, personally, do not like a line too fine for jack spinning, as in constant use winding in and out through the steel rings of the rod it is liable to be chafed flat, and might play you false when least expected or wanted. What I particularly like and recommend for this work is from 60 to 80 yards of Messrs. Allcock's No. 2 or 3 white plaited undressed silk line. These lines are very strong, the No. 2 being particularly so, and they are also very soft and free from all objectionable kinks and curls, which, I might add, is desirable, especially in a spinning line. A line that kinks and snarls in use is a confounded nuisance. I found Messrs. Allcock's (quality No. 108) lines, size 2, to be the most reliable for spinning that I ever tried. I tested one of them once with a spring balance that would weigh up to 20lb., and as it pulled this down I considered it plenty good enough without extending my experiments further in that direction. The three points noted above, viz., the judicious selection of the rod, reel, and line have more to do with the success or non-success of the angler who essays the Nottingham style of pike fishing, than some people would think; in fact, I consider it a matter of the utmost importance. I have seen men who have been utterly disheartened by repeated failures, and then found out on investigation of their particular cases that three-fourths of the causes of failure lay more in the rods, reels, and lines than in the fishermen who used them.

I hope none of my readers will consider that I have been unnecessarily tedious in treating this part of my subject and gone into details that would have been better left out. So convinced am I that this subject is not studied sufficiently that I have been led to refer to it at length. At one time I should most likely have only just skimmed the surface and glanced at it in a very cursory way, but the hundreds of questions that have been addressed to me by anglers from all parts of the country on the difficulties they

D

encounter, have told me very plainly that the information here given is of more than passing interest to the young pike fisherman. During my wanderings after sport I have seen pike fishermen at work in many and various styles, but none of them I considered to be equal to or more scientific than the Nottingham style. As I have just pointed out, this style requires an undressed or very slightly dressed and softly plaited silk line, and an easy-going and accurately running reel on purpose to successfully practise it. On the other hand, if the angler uses the live bait alone and is not tempted to spin the bait over the shallows, a waterproof line will be best for that purpose, and the easy-going and accurate character of his reel need only be a secondary consideration. Even if he does spin occasionally, preferring to do this with his fingers and with the line laid at his feet or gathered up in coils in his left hand, the waterproof line is still the best to use, and any brass, metal, or common wood reel, provided it is fairly stout—not too heavy—and large enough to hold the line, will do very well. A good waterproof line is rather an expensive item; of course there are cheap dressed lines; but in many cases these cheap lines turn out frauds of the very worst character. You cannot expect a good lasting pike line for, say, a halfpenny a yard. I never knew one yet to be up to much that could be bought for less than a penny a yard, and even some of these were nothing to crack about. I know lots of pike fishermen who prefer to buy the pure silk plaited lines and dress them themselves; but this is a long and tedious job. The cheap dressed lines, I fancy, are waterproofed with some sort of composition that has an acid mixed with it. This, I think, is done for a twofold purpose, that is, to give the line a bright and glossy appearance, and also to dry them very quickly. In some of the cheaper kinds of dressed lines this waterproofing only covers the surface, or outside of them, and rapidly peels or chips off when used for a short time; and then again I have fancied more than once that the acid used in the dressing causes the line to rot after it has been for some little time in contact with the water. If the pike fisherman prefers to buy his dressed line, or has no time on his hands to do it himself, he should see that it is of the

very best quality, for this is a case of the cheapest being
dearest in the long run ; for most assuredly a good one will
out-last three or four common ones, and a couple of shillings only at most represents the difference between sixty
yards of common dressed line and a similar length of first-
class quality. I should say that Messrs. Allcock's " Standard " waterproof line is as reliable as any that can be procured nowadays. That firm makes a speciality of these
lines, using only the purest and strongest silk and the very
best dressing procurable in their manufacture. I should not
like to say that these lines are better than other English
makers' best, but I do know from experience as a user and
dealer that they are at least equal to any others. The size
that I particularly recommend for live-baiting or coiling on
the ground is the No. 3, and as this can be procured for a
trifle more than a penny a yard, the outlay is not beyond the
reach of the generality of working men anglers. Some pike
fishermen will have it that for a pike line to be reliable you
must dress it yourself. They say that the ordinary dressed
line as usually sold in the fishing tackle shops is too stiff
and hard to comfortably use, and I am half inclined to agree
with this opinion. Anyhow, a good home-dressed line is
worth half a dozen common stiffly-dressed shop-bought ones.
To dress a line properly is a rather lengthy operation. I
don't mean lengthy as far as actual time doing the job is
concerned ; it is the length of time it takes to dry after being
soaked in the solution that makes the job so tedious. I
have known lines to be three or four months drying before
the stickiness was gone and they were fit to use. Good linseed oil—and remember it must be good, not half of it some
foreign fiery fat or other cheap adulterated stuff that is only
linseed oil in name—is as good as anything that can be
used ; and this should be mixed with an equal part of best
copal varnish, say a quarter-pint of each. One of my friends
used to also add about a couple of tablespoonfuls of best
gold size. This is a rare good dressing for a pike line, but
takes a considerable time to dry. The undressed silk line
that the angler wishes to dress should be taken when new
and perfectly dry, and coiled up into as small a ring or com-
pass as possible, say what will easily go into a small basin

four or five inches across the top; then pour the mixture as given above, cold, on top of the line and see that every portion of it is well covered. Let it remain in the dressing at least two days, then carefully remove and uncoil it, and with a bit of flannel wipe it gently from one end to the other; that is, hold the flannel between the finger and thumb of the left hand, and with the right draw the line through, taking care that the pressure is sufficient to remove all lumps and superfluous dressing from the line—of course during the process the line can be coiled on a table or round the back of a chair. It should then be hung up in long loose coils in a cool dry position, and where the sun does not shine on it, and remain there until perfectly dry; I should say it will take six or eight weeks at the very least to properly dry. This dressing not only has the merit of being very good, but it also is cheap, any respectable chemist or oilman will supply sufficient of the ingredients to dress a couple of lines for eightpence or tenpence, I make no doubt. After the line has hung until dry it should be stretched out at full length down the garden path, or any other convenient situation, and a sixpenny packet of " King's Ceroleum " procured, this is another very useful line dressing, and is sold at nearly any fishing tackle shop; a bit about the size of a filbert nut should be put inside a bit of flannel and rubbed lightly from end to end of the line, taking care that a very thin coat only covers the whole surface; now take another bit of dry flannel and polish up the line smartly, pinch it well between finger and thumb and rub backwards and forwards, a yard at a time, until the line feels warm between your fingers, this gives the finishing touch to the dressing and smooths the line down with a slight gloss. The dressing will not crack or chip off, nor is it hard and stiff in the slightest, but so soft and pliable that it can be thrown very well from the reel in the Nottingham syle. A great friend of mine, one of the very best pike fishermen I ever knew, always maintained that a line dressed according to the directions just given, had a threefold lease of life given it, it would outlast three ordinary undressed or even cheaped dressed ones and so be a considerable saving in the long run. I think I have made it perfectly clear as to the ingredients required for this dressing, but to make it doubly sure, I might say, that my friend always got a quarter pint each of best linseed oil and copal varnish, and two tablespoonfulls of best gold size, mixing and stirring them well together before pouring over the lines. This quantity being quite sufficient for two eighty yard lengths. If the gold size cannot be procured, it does not matter so much, but still we always fancied it gave the line a more finished appearance; and don't forget the finishing touches with " King's Ceroleum " and flannel. After this it should again be hung up for two or three days before finally wound on the reel. I might add that the long or short life of a pike line depends on more than a careful dressing, it should also be thoroughly dried after using, and by having good steel snake rings and steel end rings on the rod, also contribute to its long life. There are several more ways of dressing a line, such as putting it in a mixture of beeswax, resin, and boiled oil; or melting a lump of solid parrafin and dropping in the line; but the first that I have given at length will be found enough for all practical purposes. Personally, as I generally throw direct from the reel, in either spinning or livebaiting, I don't care much about having a dressed line; but there is no question that the great bulk of pike fishermen find a dressed line of the very greatest convenience, particularly in casting out and working a live bait. Once or twice during a busy season I have rubbed my spinning line with a little bit of " King's Ceroleum," and found it helped to preserve it, besides making it stand the wear and tear of constantly running through the rings of the rod somewhat better, and also preventing it from getting quite so much waterlogged while in use. This is the very outside that I care about, in the shape of a waterproof or dressed line, and as this preparation is so easy in its application, and can be put on so quickly, and does not alter the softness and flexibility of the line, the novice will find it to be to his advantage if he keeps a cake of this dressing by him; the cost is only sixpence, and I think it is kept by most fishing tackle dealers, but if any difficulty is experienced in procuring it, a note to the inventor, Mr. Wm. King, chemist, Ipswich, will, I make no doubt, result in a satisfactory reply. I used to stretch my

line at full length in the most convenient situation, and
smartly rub a small piece of the ceroleum with the help of
a bit of flannel from end to end, taking care that very little
was put one, and this rubbed well in till the whole surface
was smooth and bright. The line was then hung up for
a couple of days, after which interval it was safe to use; I
found that this very slight dressing did not hinder the free
running of the line when thrown direct from the reel in
the Nottingham style. Of course three or four coats of
this preparation can be applied in the same manner, at intervals of a couple of days between each one, if the angler
wishes to have his line more thickly and thoroughly waterproof. This does not take anything like so long drying as
the oil and varnish dressing mentioned some time ago; a
week after applying the last coat will be ample. And now
having looked at what I consider to be the very beau ideal
of a pike rod, reel, line, and its dressing, we will glance
briefly at one or two sundries that the pike fisherman should
have if he can anyhow afford them. One of the most important is a line dryer, because it is imperative that the pike

FIG. 4. THE LINE DRIER.

line should be dried after you get home from a day's fishing,
or if you are foolish enough to neglect it, in all probability
you will have a sudden and startling reminder during one
of your subsequent outings, sooner or later. The line will
rot if allowed to dry on the reel time after time, and the fish
of the season may be hooked and lost. There is nothing

more annoying than to have a good fish break away owing
to the line being rotten by neglect. The accompanying
illustration gives a good idea of what a line dryer is like;
it has a clamp on one side near the centre, so that it can be
screwed to the edge of a table, or the bench, or the chimney
piece, and a handle on the other side to wind the line off
the reel. I daresay any handy man could soon knock up a
similar article, anyhow the expense is not very much, and
most decidedly it is not a useless expense. I should unwind
the whole of the line from the reel, and put the drier some-
where in a dry, cool position, and let it remain a couple of
days if you anyhow can, before winding back again on the
reel. Even if you are out in a strange place for two or three
days' jack fishing, the line will be all the better for being
dried every night and wound again on the reel next morning.
On no account should a line be dried in close proximity
to a fire, particularly a dressed line, as the heat may blister
the waterproofing and cause a weakness.

Another actual necessity in a pike fisherman's kit is a
good landing net, or a gaff hook; I prefer the former, and
this I recommend to be of pretty substantial build. A
strong four jointed folding iron frame, or ring of a circular

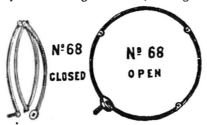

FIG. 5. FOLDING LANDING RING.

shape not less than sixteen inches in diameter, being, in my
opinion, the best to employ. This ring should screw firmly
and tight into a socket fixed at the end of a staff, the staff
or handle can be about four and a half feet long, and made
of good East India mottled cane, and if it is made large
enough, so that when it is bored out it will hold the rod top

that is just then not in use, it will be found a great
convenience. The illustration shows a ring I recommend
open for use, and also closed for convenience of carriage.
With regard to the net itself it should be fairly strong, and
the material barked or tanned, and it will be all the better
if it is pretty deep, say from twenty-one to twenty-four
inches, and roomy at the bottom, so that when a jack gets
inside it is likely to stop in; because if you are spinning
with a number of hooks on your flight and get a jack into
the net, if this net is narrow at the bottom and shallow, he
will most likely roll out again; and if the hooks of the
flight catch inside the net while the pike is hanging outside,
you stand a very good chance of bidding him a good bye
within the next two seconds, for most assuredly he will
speedily shake himself free. Some good pike fishermen,
on account of the extreme likelihood of this accident hap-
pening when landing a pike in a net, prefer to use a gaff
hook for this purpose, striking it into the fish near the
shoulder or under the gills; but I have known a good pike
to twist a gaff clean out of the hands of a fisherman, and
at least once or twice I have known the gaff hook to snap
off at the bend, and the pike escape with the broken portion

075

GAFF HOOK, OPEN AND CLOSED.

sticking in him. The illustration shows the usual sort of
gaff that is most in use, open for use, and also closed for
convenience of carriage; but, taking things all round, I
most certainly prefer a good strong landing net, wide at the
bottom and pretty deep. Another very useful article is a
tackle case, and this should be of japanned tin, black on the
outside, enamelled white on the inside, and made with several partitions, so that traces and flights can be kept seper-
ate. A good useful size is about eight inches long by five
wide, and about one and a half inches thick, with two closed
boxes in the lid for traces. A tin box is better for pike

tackle than a leather case, as in the latter the treble hooks are liable to be broken if anything heavy is thrown on the case. The annexed drawing shows one of these tackle cases

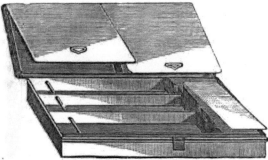

FIG. 7. BOX FOR PIKE TACKLE.

open, so that the inside arrangements can be seen. A strong canvas haversack of a pretty fair size is also another useful article, particularly if the pike fisherman goes in for a good deal of spinning, as it can be slung across his shoulders, and so out of the way while at work with his spinning bait, and does not have to be picked up and carried in the hand to every fresh place he wishes to try. A pike fisherman should also always have a bottle of varnish handy at home, as it is very useful for a variety of purposes, the best that I know for pike tackle being two pennyworth of the wood naphtha, in a doctor's medicine bottle, with two ounces of best brown shellac dissolved in it. Wood naphtha is far better than spirits of wine, as the latter evaporates, and after being some time on the bindings or whipping of rod or tackle the gum rubs off like a dry dust. The bindings of all pike tackle should be from time to time painted over thinly and lightly with a little of the before mentioned mixture; a small camels hair brush being the best for this purpose. This small brush should always be kept in a little of the naphtha in a separate bottle or vessel, or if allowed to get dry the bristles would be as hard as a bit of stick. I am certain it will pay the angler to touch up his tackle pretty frequently, as it helps to keep the bindings secure, and doubles the life of it. A little good carriage maker's varnish is the best for his rod, painted lightly and thinly over the surface, but this should only be done at the end of a season, when it could stand on one side for a week or two and get thoroughly hard and dry. Finally, I might say, that the pike fisherman who values his health should always, in bad weather, wear good waterproof boots or shoes, and keep them well dressed with " Dale's dubbin." The various flights and tackles for spinning and livebaiting; how to make and how to use them, will be illustrated as far as practicable, and described in the chapters that follow.

CHAPTER III.

THE PIKE *(continued)*.

Different methods of casting—The Nottingham style—The right-handed cast—The cast from the left hand—How to cast from the reel—Weights and their distribution—The forward swing—Casting with a coiled line—A peculiar cast.

In this chapter I propose to leave the beaten track for awhile, saying nothing about the merits or demerits of the various flights and tackles in use for pike fishing, but devote the whole of it to a subject that I think has hardly ever been satisfactorily explained—I allude to the question of properly casting out a bait. There seems to me to be two or three different schools of fishermen, each throwing out the bait in its own particular fashion, each more or less proficient in its own peculiar style, and all of them suited up to a certain point to the requirements of the various waters in which they ply their craft. As I hinted in the previous chapter, there are those who coil the line at their feet, casting the bait from the rod point; but this, in my opinion, is not likely to be an unqualified success when tried in every conceivable situation, and under every condition, and in all the difficulties to be encountered by the side of the river, lake, or stream. Then again there are others who never use the rod when casting out a pike bait, they simply coil a lot of line on the ground, with the rod on rests, hanging the bait in the crutch of a forked stick, and so slinging it out without the aid of the rod at all. Then again there is the ever increasing army of casters who throw directly from the reel in what is known as the Nottingham style. In my opinion this style is far away and above any other, taking all things into consideration ; places can be successfully spun over where it would be impossible, owing to stones, bushes, trees, reeds, and rank undergrowth, to cast with line coiled at the feet. Some pike fishermen say that a bait, wound home on the reel in this style, is not so attractive as one worked home by the fingers with line coiled; the long sweeping drags of the bait when travelling through the water, which is the chief characteristic of the latter plan, is absent when the line is simply wound up on the reel to spin the bait home. There is, they say, too much of the jog trot, monotonous sameness about the bait when cast out and wound back again direct from the reel. But I would point out that by simply raising and lowering alternately the tip end of the rod, and varying the pace of the winding in process, sometimes even, if the character of the water permitted it pausing for a second or so, the sink and draw motion and the long sweeping drags of the bait could be imitated as faithfully with the reel, as by the hand. Then again, when spinning from a boat the line when coiled at the feet is apt to be a confounded nuisance, and will insist on catching round everything within reach, now and again

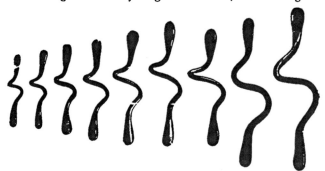

FIG. 8. SNAKE RINGS, THE FOUR LARGEST SIZES RIGHT FOR A CASTING ROD.

hanking round the neck of a bottle, or upsetting a tackle box, perhaps throwing overboard a cherished pocket knife or a favourite bit of tackle. I have heard several pike fishermen say under these circumstances, that they wished they could spin from the reel, as it would prevent much bad

language to say the very least. As I have hinted more than
once in the foregoing pages, that my favourite plan of spinning is by casting out the bait direct from the reel, I will
commence with that and trust I shall be able to make it so
clear that even the most inexperienced angler will have no
difficulty in understanding exactly what I mean, but be able,
after a little practise, to perform in a very creditable manner, without any serious mishaps. Of course he will not be
able to do it all at once, he is bound to jerk his bait off the
hooks some odd times, and also find after an unsuccessful
attempt that his line has managed to get into a beautiful
tangle on the barrel of his reel. The greatest difficulty
that I have to contend with, is the fact that it is almost
impossible to lay down a hard and fast line as to how the
rod and reel should be manipulated in casting out a pike
bait, in what is known as the "Nottingham style." Even
experts are by no means agreed on the subject; and so on
looking at it by the light of many years practical experience,
and also calling to mind the various plans adopted by some
of my personal friends who, in their own way of throwing
out a bait in this style, are as good fishermen as ever threw
across river, lake, or stream, I say again that no fixed rule
can be laid down, as some men check the reel with the
right hand, others with the left. All men are not alike, the
plan that is free and easy to one may be difficult and even
painful to another; he must throw in the fashion that is
easiest to himself, and to get into the fashion that is easiest
can only be acquired after very careful practice. I have
seen anglers whom nobody who knew them, and understood
the matter, could by any means call inexperienced fishermen, cast out the bait with the right hand above the reel,
and the fingers of the left guarding the revolving barrel at the
top edge, and I have also seen as equally good and as long
experienced men proceeding exactly opposite, with the left
hand above the reel and the right below it, guarding the
reel at the bottom edge. Each of these plans is equally
as good as the other; that is, so far as throwing out the
bait, and checking the speed of the reel at the proper
moment is concerned. A man must find out which is the
easiest and the most accurate of the two plans, that he, per-

sonally, with the most comfort to himself, can adopt, and
then he will be in a fair way to success, no matter which of
the two he selects. The plan that I found to be the easiest
for myself is what is known as the right-handed cast. This
is a cast that is adopted by many first class men in various
parts of the kingdom; men who, as it were, graduated on
the Trent, and then left their native river to settle on the
banks of other waters, carrying their style to places where it
was practically unknown before. I have heard it said that
the introduction of this style to various well known rivers,
marked a new era in the history of their angling. In the
first place the angler must find out exactly where to hold
his rod so as to have the best command over it. It will not
do for him to hold it in a careless manner, he must be
master of his rod—and not the rod master of him—or in
all probability he will land his bait into the nearest hedge
instead of on the water. The proper right-handed cast is
made by grasping the rod firmly with the right hand, about
eight or nine inches above the narrow stop ring, or band of
the winch-fittings. This small stop ring or band, by the
way, should be firmly fixed on the rod butt, about an inch
above the slot that is cut into the wood to receive the reel.
When this reel is put on the rod in its proper position, the
two handles should be pointing to the right. The right
hand, as I have just said grasps the rod firmly, nine or ten
inches above the reel; the left hand is close over the reel
or winch fittings, in fact, to be exact, the rod is in the hollow between the thumb and forefinger of the left hand, close
to the reel, so that the fingers of the left hand can clasp the
back of the reel, the second finger reaching over the barrel
and just lightly touching the rim of the front or revolving
plate of the barrel on the top edge. By this plan you are
out of the way of the handles, and in no danger of being
smartly rapped over the fingers by them. After seeing that
your bait hangs some four or five feet from the point of
the rod—but this is regulated by the length of the trace—on
no account should any of the gimp or gut, whichever is used,
be wound through the top ring of the rod before making
the cast. The flight of hooks, the leaded trace, and the loop
where the silk line is joined to the trace, should all hang

free below the top ring on rod. After seeing that all is
clear, you face exactly the place on the water where you
want the bait to drop; keep your eyes fixed on the exact
spot where you would like that bait to strike the water,
never mind looking at the bait just when the cast has com-
menced, if all is clear, it will look after itself very well. To
make the cast you swing the rod point to your right-hand
side and partly behind you; then with another, but this
time a much more smarter forward swing, you bring the rod
over the water. As soon as ever the bait swings forward
you partly release the reel by easing the pressure of your
finger on the revolving front rim, taking care, however, that
this pressure is not altogether removed, or the reel will over-
run, and also minding at the same time that this pressure is
not too tight, or the bait will be checked and drop on the
bank to your left hand. Your finger should just feel the
rim of the reel, and that is all. As soon as the bait strikes
the water the finger is pressed tight on the reel edge, so as
to effectually stop any further revolutions. Still keeping
hold of the rod and reel with the left hand close at the top
of the reel, as already described, you press the knob or button of the rod into the hollow of the left thigh, and leave go
of the rod with the right hand, which hand is brought down
and takes hold of the reel handles on purpose to wind the
bait home again. With a little practice these three opera-
tions can be performed in a couple of seconds with the ease
and regularity of clockwork, viz., stopping the reel by a pressure of the finger as soon as the bait drops into the water,
pressing the butt end of the rod into the hollow of the thigh,
and leaving go with the right hand (which in making the
cast was 9 or 10 inches above the reel) in order to wind in
the bait. This is what I call the proper right-handed cast;
in fact, by this plan I can cast the bait to the right hand or
to the left, or even straight forward, although in the case of
a bait being required to be thrown wide to the right hand, I
usually bring my rod over the left shoulder instead of the
right, as described before; but in any of the three directions
I hold rod and reel in the same hand and in the same manner. In this right-handed cast the most natural direction
for the bait to travel is wide to the left hand, in a slanting

direction across the river. It requires some practice before
a given point in any direction can be successfully, time after
time, struck.   Some very good Nottingham pike fishermen
that I know always make what I call a left-handed cast; the
rod is grasped with the left hand just above the reel, and
the right hand below it, checking the speed of the reel with
the end of a finger at the bottom edge.   But with all due
respect I maintain that this is a very awkward throw, because ere you can wind up your reel to spin the bait home
both hands have to be shifted, the left lower down to have
command over the rod and the right to wind in the reel
line; and if the place spun over happens to be shallow and
weedy this extra fraction of time may make all the difference
between the bait being clear and the hooks catching hold of
the weeds just under the surface.   Again, I always imagine
that the finger under the reel does not regulate the cast so
well as the finger over the top, and you are more liable to
get your fingers rapped by the revolving handles.   It is more
than probable that you may sometimes stand facing the
river in a very awkward position, with a lot of boughs or
other obstructions immediately at your right hand, and no
possible chance of swinging the rod point in that direction.
Under these conditions no other cast except the left-handed
one is possible.   But even here I should hold the rod and
check the reel exactly the same as for the right-handed cast,
the only difference being that the rod point would be swung
towards the left hand instead of towards the right.   It is
much more difficult to make a clean and accurate cast from
the left shoulder than it is from the right.   I have known
very good pike spinners who threw out the bait in a manner
peculiar to themselves.   Not one angler in a dozen could,
if they tried for a month, imitate it.   I don't condemn all
these styles, far from it.   If a man can throw out his bait
well and accurately, and his style of throwing is to my eye
very peculiar, I should say nothing in condemnation because
that style differed widely from my own.   One of the most
curious throwers that I ever saw was a Nottinghamshire
angler of long and wide experience.   He always used to put
the reel on his rod with the handles pointing to the left,
and wind in his line with the left hand.   His style was

peculiar in the extreme, but his worst enemy (if he had one) could not say that he was a bad thrower. Personally, in giving practical lessons in this style, I found that the greater number of my pupils could manage the right-handed cast much quicker and easier than any other; but it needs practise, and practice alone, to make a man perfectly master of the style. But there is one comforting thought in the whole business, it is as easy as A B C when you once know how, and it is not at all difficult to learn. The main thing to be observed and impressed most strongly upon the would-be spinner, is to grip the rod firmly with the right hand the proper distance above the reel, and with the fingers of the left regulate the speed of the revolving barrel, and he should also bear in mind most strongly that while the bait is travelling towards its destination, the slight pressure of the finger on the edge of the reel must always be there, regulated according to size of bait and weight of lead. If a heavy natural bait a little more pressure must be applied, and if it is a light artificial bait a little less pressure will be ample, as a light bait takes more force than a heavy one to start it upon its journey. In using a natural bait, say a small dace of from one-and-a-half to two ounces in weight, a gentle throw with an easy swing will be all that is required to get it out a moderate distance, say from 25 to 30 yards, provided the reel is an easy-running one and the line moderately fine. It is not advisable to exercise tremendous force in casting out a natural bait, for various reasons; not much would be gained in the distance cast for one thing, and a sudden jerk, which is always liable to happen when extra force is applied, might buckle up and spoil the shape of the bait. I found on several occasions that the longest cast was made with the easiest swing, that is when bait has been fairly heavy. On the other hand a light lead and small artificial bait of not more than one ounce in weight altogether would have to be started much smarter upon its journey— more force is necessary in this instance. The gentle throw or swing that would be ample in the case of a very heavy bait would not cause the reel to commence running with sufficient speed for the light bait to travel the requisite distance.

E

But all these points cannot be learned very well from reading about them; a hint or two, of course, that will be useful to the novice can be given. For all the rest, such as holding the rod in the best place, easing or checking the reel with the ends of the fingers in the best manner, the proper distance for the bait to hang below the rod point, and the correct swing to give the rod, in order for each individual spinner to have the best and easiest results, can only be acquired by long and painstaking trials and experiments. But don't be frightened, peg away, and you will soon learn. One man of my acquaintance who knew nothing whatever about this style, but was anxious to learn, made such rapid progress during his first lesson that at the end of an hour he could cast out 30 yards without jerk, tangle, or catch. There is one little thing I should like to say here before I forget it, and that is, when making a cast, and the bait has travelled nearly to its destination, lower the rod point to about a couple of feet from the surface of the water, if the nature of the place makes it anyhow possible to be done. More particularly must this be observed if the place spun over be shallow and weedy and the angler not very proficient in recovering his line to wind home again. As soon as the bait strikes the water, the rod point can be raised, and this will keep the bait on the surface, and the hooks not be so liable to catch hold of the weeds until the winding-in process commences. And now just a few words as to the weight that can comfortably be thrown and the distance that can be cast.

Careful trials with various reels and lines have shown me very clearly that a small feather-weight minnow, without any lead on the trace, cannot be thrown direct from the reel and rod.point. The smallest weight that I found possible to cast over 20 yards was a small spoon which, with its lead and gimp trace, weighed three-quarters of an ounce, this weight being distributed as follows:—The spoon at the extreme end of two feet of fine gimp; at this distance from the spoon was a small barrel lead, then two more feet of gimp, the whole of these weighing as just stated; and even this wanted a No. 4 line and a Coxon reel to do it with. The ordinary pike reel and line was not equal to the task. A

larger spoon and heavier leaded trace, with weight distributed as before, the whole weighing a little less than one-
and-a-quarter ounces, was next tried with the ordinary reel
and No. 2 line, and this time by using some considerable
force in the cast I managed to get it out about 30 yards.
The result of my experiments convinced me that the bait
with its necessary swivels, gimp trace, and lead, the whole
distributed in a proper manner, and not put altogether at
the far end of the gimp, should weigh not less than one and
a half ounces to have a comfortable and satisfactory result,
that is if distance and accuracy were the objects aimed at.
A leger bullet weighing seven-eighths of an ounce, tied
firmly at the end of a stout barbel line, was thrown a little
over 50 yards from the reel, while a spoon and leaded trace
weighing one and a half ounces only reached 40 yards when
thrown by the same rod, reel, and line. The bullet, of
course, would have far less resistance to contend with in
travelling through the air than would the spoon, hence the
difference between the distances cast under the same conditions. A small dace weighing from one and a half ounces
to two and a quarter ounces can be comfortably thrown without any danger of straining the rod; anything much over
the latter weight is not desirable. With regard to the distance that can be cast direct from the reel, I should say that
60 yards would be the very outside, and then the bait would
have to be fairly heavy, and of such a torpedo-like shape
that it could cut through the air with the least possible resistance, and the conditions of the weather would also have
to be very favourable. I have heard some men say that
they have cast out the bait from the reel 70, and even 80,
yards at a guess; but I must say that I have never seen it
done yet. If they had the distance properly measured I am
afraid they would find it considerably shorter than that.
Shortly then, we may put it that 50 yards is a very long cast,
40 yards is a very good one indeed, while in a day's spinning
there would be more casts under 30 yards than over that
figure, that is as far as the ordinary run of mankind is concerned. I once saw some Thames professional fishermen
competing for prizes by casting out an artificial bait from the
reel in a style that they were pleased to call the Nottingham

style.   Instead of swinging the rod to the right hand or to the left, and propelling the bait forward by a gentle side cast, two or three of them handled the rod a good deal like a country labourer using a frail.   They grasped the rod with one hand above the reel, and the other below it, and swung the point and bait over their heads straight behind them, so that the rod was in a direct line with the middle of their backs, and both hands at the back of the head.   In making the cast the rod was brought smartly forward with the point high in the air; in fact, the rod described a semi-circle, or very nearly so; and such was the force of this terrific cast that the bait travelled to a great height before dropping on the ground.   This cast, if applied to actual pike fishing with a tender natural bait, would result in dire disaster to the bait, at any rate; it would be thrown all to atoms in two casts.   The gentle side swing with the finger on the edge of the reel is the correct and proper style, that is if your baits are scarce and you want them to keep attractive as long as possible.   Of course it does not matter so much with a strong metal artificial bait how it is thrown, so long as it goes out to the best advantage.   Sometimes you may stand in a very awkward position among trees or bushes, where it is impossible to swing the rod point to either side, or even upwards; there is perhaps no more than two or three yards of clear space immediately fronting the spot on which you stand.   Under these circumstances a very creditable cast can be made by drawing down a length of line from between the rings of the rod as high up as you can reach, and letting the bait swing backwards and forwards by moving the rod point as far upwards and downwards as the circumstances of the place will allow.   When the bait has acquired sufficient momentum and swings sharply forward, release the loop of line that you hold in the left hand, which has been drawn down from between the rings on the rod, and at the same time ease the pressure of the little finger of the right hand on the edge of the reel, and away goes the bait, the weight of which will cause the reel to revolve sufficiently to get out 20 yards, at the very least, if it is wanted.   In this cast the rod must be held in the right hand above the reel, with the edge or side of the little finger resting lightly on the top edge of the revolving barrel. When this cast is made and the bait strikes the water, change the rod from the right hand to the left as quickly and promptly as possible, and wind home again, repeating the process as often as required.

One of the very best casters that I ever saw throw out a pike bait had his line hanging in coils from his left hand; his right hand grasped the rod some little distance above a brass winch; his right arm and body acted as a fulcrum in a very peculiar manner, so that he had the most possible leverage and power with his rod at the least expenditure of strength. It was marvellous to see the way those coils of line straightened themselves out one after another and went through the rings of the rod as the bait flew with unerring accuracy to the exact spot required. Nor was it much less marvellous to see the way that line recoiled itself in regular sized folds on his left hand as the bait was spun home. That man's skill could only have been arrived at by long and constant practise, as I never saw him all that afternoon make a false cast or get his line into the least semblance of a tangle.

Before the introduction of the Nottingham style on the Thames and the southern rivers, the great majority of the pike fishermen on those waters used to cast with the line coiled at the feet, and certainly some of the experts in this style can throw out a wonderful distance. There is no question that so far as distance is concerned a first-class Thames-style man will beat the Nottingham-style man by at least a dozen yards, using the same weight; in fact I have seen it demonstrated more than once at those popular bait-casting tournaments held at intervals at the Welsh Harp, Twickenham, and Wimbledon, when the very best exponents of both styles have been competitors. In this style the bait is thrown direct from the rod point, only instead of the line being wound on the reel it is laid in loose coils on the ground. Of course the line as it picks itself off the ground travels through the rings on the rod during the flight of the bait, and when it is spun home again it is drawn in by hand and again laid in coils at the angler's feet. But with all due respect to the many excellent Thames men I don't consider the plan half so neat and clean as casting direct from the

reel, for the reasons stated at the commencement of this
chapter.   The pike fishermen of the Welsh Harp seem to
me to have a plan of throwing out a bait peculiar to themselves.   In this case the line does not travel through the
rings of the rod.   Like the Thames style, the line itself lays
in coils at the angler's feet; but instead of using the rod as
the motive power of the cast, the bait, or at least the line
about a yard from the bait, is hung across a steel or brass
fork that is screwed firmly into the end of a staff like a landing handle, and it is marvellous the distance an expert can
cast the bait, that is if line and all is clear and goes freely.
Another plan of casting out a bait that I have sometimes
seen is by having the line wound tightly on the left hand,
each fold of the line crossing the previous one, the hand
itself being moved in a peculiar manner as the line is coiled
on and the bait spun home.   When the cast is made direct
from the rod point, the line unwinds itself off the angler's
hand and passes through the rings on the rod.   When the
bait has reached its destination and is travelling home again,
the peculiar motion of the hand that gathers in the line fold
over fold causes the bait to travel in a manner that could
not be imitated by any other plan.   It is a wonderfully
killing style, and is adopted by some of the best minnow
spinners for trout, as well as certain pike fishermen who de-
light to spin with a very small bait and fine lines and tackle.

CHAPTER IV.

THE PIKE *(continued).*

SPINNING WITH A NATURAL BAIT.

Spinning, what it is—A simple spinning tackle—The Chapman spinner and its contemporaries—Flights and their uses—The spinning trace—Best baits for spinning—" The Trent Otter's" spinning flight—How to bait it—A good season—How to spin to have the best results—Different methods for different waters—Condition of the water—Clouded v. clear water spinning—Spinning in deep and sluggish waters—Changing the bait—Striking, playing, and landing a pike—Haunts of the pike during the Different months—Spinning leads—Preserving dead baits.

Spinning for pike with a natural or artificial bait has been a favourite pastime of mine for many years now; in fact I look upon spinning as being the most scientific as well as the most sportsmanlike of all the many plans that are adopted for the capture of our fresh-water shark. Of course, I am aware that there are certain waters containing pike in which it would be utterly impossible to work a spinning bait, or even for the matter of that a live bait. Obstructions and weeds might be so strongly and thickly in evidence that the novice would despair of ever getting a bait in, to say nothing of safely getting it out again. I shall show presently how it is possible to fish a place like that; for the present my object is to give a few plain instructions on spinning over the more open waters with a dead natural bait.

I suppose I need not tell the amateur that spinning is done by fixing a small fish on an arrangement of hooks in such a manner that when drawn through the water it looks like a wounded or disabled fish trying to escape from some imaginary foe, the main object being to have as much of the bait and as little as possible of the hooks visible. The spinning bait must also be kept constantly moving, that is, turning over and over more or less slowly or rapidly, as the case may be, during its passage back to the angler after being thrown out. Spinning is hard work if stuck to all day long, for it is absolutely necessary to be on the move throwing out and winding home again time after time. It won't do to let the bait sink to the bottom and stay there for any length of time. Spinning is working the bait all over the place, anyhow and anywhere, wherever there is a bit of clear water into which it can be thrown. A friend who had never done any fishing except a little bit of roaching once or twice with a tight line, had a curious idea about spinning. He was staying with a farmer friend who had a bit of very fair pike water running through his grounds. The farmer rigged him up on the second morning of his stay with a strong rod, reel, line, trace, and a spoon bait, all fitted up and ready, and told him he could amuse himself spinning for an hour or two, till he had time to join him. Some two or three hours later the farmer went down to see how he was getting on, and was considerably astonished to find him with the rod laid across a bed of weeds, the line in the water, and blowing a cloud of tobacco smoke into the air as contentedly as possible. He had actually thrown the spoon bait into the water, allowed it to sink to the bottom, laid the rod across the weeds, and had been waiting all that time for a bite.

A glance through a wholesale manufacturer's illustrated catalogue would be enough to convince the veriest novice that the making of artificial baits and spinning tackles for pike fishing had brought out the ingenuity of the maker to a remarkable degree. The almost endless variety there displayed would be to the tyro, as our old friend Dick Swiveller used to say, " a staggerer." Of the merits and demerits of the various forms of artificial baits, from the old-fashioned spoon to the elaborately gilded and fish-shaped article that spins through the water like one line of glittering silver, I will not just now touch upon, but reserve that subject for another chapter. My business now is to briefly look at those tackles that are used for spinning a natural or dead bait, and see wherein and under what conditions of shape and spinning powers the most sport is likely to be had.

I am old enough to remember one of the old school of

Trent anglers who lived at Newark-on-Trent, who used to
spin for pike in a manner that I should suppose to be a sur-
vival of the most ancient form of trolling known. This old
angler's name was Crosby, and there are fishermen still living at Newark who can very well remember him. He used
neither rod nor reel, but simply a coil of very stout cord,
about as thick, I should say, as a sea-fishing hand-line, which
he carried in his left hand, with one end tied tightly round
the same arm above the elbow. His tackle was simply a
length of stout gimp with one or two large swivels, and a
long heavy pipe or barrel lead. The gimp was mounted
with one only very large treble hook, and this gimp was
threaded through the bait, the hook being underneath between the vent and the tail. This tackle was thrown by
hand, and in spinning the bait home the line was drawn in
by the right hand and laid in coils on the left. Of course
all fish hooked had to be played by hand. I cannot remember seeing this angler at work myself, but I knew him very
well, and have been assured by old fishermen that years ago
he used to kill many and heavy fish by that very primitive
style and tackle. There are many tackles in use for spinning a dead bait that are a good deal more ingenious than
useful, that is some of them, at least are so. The main
object of the inventors of these tackles appears to be a desire
to save the angler from being at any trouble in the matter,
and also to secure a very brilliant and even spin. One of
the oldest of these is the Chapman spinner, which I should
say is familiar to anglers in every part of the civilized globe
where fish that will take a spinning bait are to be found.
For the information of those who don't know what it is, I
may say that it has a leaded brass wire with a hook some
two-thirds of the distance down it, which is thrust in the
mouth and down the belly of the bait. At the top of the
leaded wire, close to the mouth of the bait, there are sol-
dered on a couple of fans, one being bent one way and the
other in an opposite direction, somewhat on the Archimedean screw principle, that gives the bait its rotary movement
without having to curl the tail. A swivel is fixed at the top
end above these projecting fans, from which depends a
couple of short lengths of gimp ; two treble hooks are firmly

whipped on the longest length of gimp, and one on the
shortest length, the two hooks being on one side of the
bait, and the odd one on the opposite side, one hook of each
treble being stuck in the bait in such a manner that the odd
treble is about midway between the other two, only, of
course, on opposite sides. I have had my attention drawn
to lots of these spinning tackles that are known by various
names, and brought out by various makers, but the whole
of them seem to take the old-fashioned Chapman as a
model, and are only imitations and improvements of that

FIG. 9. THE ARCHER SPINNER, STANDARD PATTERN.

good old spinner. There is the Bedford spinner, the Archer
spinner, Gregory's Archimedean spinner, the Angler's spinner, and a whole host of others, some differing in the shape
of the hook, others differing slightly in the blade that is
thrust down the belly; while others again have the contrivance that fastens the bait firmly, slightly different to other
makers. But look at them all, you will find the method of
mounting to be nearly similar in every respect, and the old-
fashioned Chapman to be strongly in evidence in nearly
everyone of them. The Coxon spinner is about the simplest
of the lot; but it is not an unqualified success in any and
all conditions of streams and waters. It is a capital spinner
when tried down the heavy waters of the Trent, and kills a
fair percentage of the pike it hooks; but when used in very
quiet waters, where the jack take a spinning bait in a much
more quiet and deliberate manner than they do in a rapid
stream, the percentage of losses is very great indeed, and
its action as a spinner is not so good as might be desired. I
fancy it would be better if instead of having only two trebles
both on one side of the bait, it had an extra one high up
near the shoulder on the opposite side. Several friends

have tried this spinner at my earnest request in various
waters of the kingdom, and the majority of them say that
the idea is a good one. It wants improving in one or two
particulars to make it suitable for still-water spinning, and
then it would be about as perfect as it is possible to get a
spinning tackle. My own opinion is that the two trebles are
fixed too far apart; they should be nearly close together at
the tail end of the bait, with a reversed single hook near the
shoulder to keep the gimp in its position close to the bait,
and an additional treble on the opposite side nearer the head
than tail. Anyhow my experience with spinning tackles has
shown me very plainly that the best results have been ob-
tained by having the trebles distributed over the bait in this
manner. And even now, on looking at the improved Coxon
as just suggested we again find that the old-fashioned Chap-
man-like method of mounting has become strongly in evidence, the only difference being that the unsightly fans that
are close to the head of the bait in the Chapman are absent
in the Coxon, the blade of the latter that goes down the
belly of the bait, being bent by the fingers after baiting to

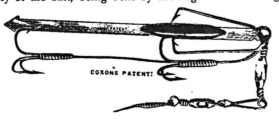

FIG. 10. THE COXON SPINNER.

give the rotary or spinning movement. I personally do not
care very much for any of these elaborately-made spinners,
preferring to mount my bait on a simple flight of hooks and
trusting to these hooks and the shape of the bait to secure
the most attractive spin. There is, however, one thing to
be said in favour of these spinners, and that is, a bait will
last longer on them than it will when mounted on an
ordinary flight. I know some very good men of the
old-fashioned school of Trent anglers who to this day
spin that river with only one large sized treble hook fixed

on the end of a length of gimp, which gimp is threaded
right through the bait from the vent to the mouth, and kill
fish on it, too. Others, again, use two trebles threaded in the
same manner. I very seldom saw more than two trebles on
a spinning flight used down that river. In nine cases out of
ten the pike of those fast streams would grab the bait near
the tail, while in a lake or very slow running stream they
would seize it in a much more deliberate manner, and generally crossways nearer the head, necessitating a slightly different tackle to what is so effective down the Trent. Some
anglers seem to consider that it is also the correct thing for
a spinning bait to travel at a very fast rate through the
water, and to spin brilliantly and evenly, so that when drawn
through the water it appears to travel in one straight and
even line ; my own experience is not in favour of this theory.
A pike, although a greedy fish, does not like too much
trouble in capturing his prey. A small fish in difficulties,
or one wounded, is far more likely to be the victim than a
dace or small chub in the full power of its strength and
swiftness. I find that a spinning bait which travels in all
sorts of curious ways to be the most attractive; in fact, as
just said, the more it looks like a disabled and wounded fish
the more likely is the jack to follow it. A dace in full
health and strength when startled will shoot through the
water like a flash, and Mr. Pike has sense enough to know
that it is a lot of trouble to openly pursue that quarry, whereas a wounded one in trying to swim away from danger will
turn from side to side and make all sorts of curious curves
and twists in its endeavours to reach a place of safety. In
my opinion and experience I find that the nearer we can ap-
proach this motion the more likely are we to attract
the attention of the pike. Some spinning flights are made
with three or four treble hooks and fixed in the bait all down
one side ; and most likely these hooks are three or four sizes
too big. In a flight of this description it is very nearly
necessary that the bait should turn over rapidly, so that the
rank arming of hooks is not presented too glaring to the
pike. I have never yet found that large sized hooks and
too many of them are an advantage, rather the reverse. I
have often wondered why the makers of tackle should re-

commend these treble hooks for spinning to be so big. The simpler the flight the more chance has the spinner, especially on those days when the pike are not in a very taking humour. Sometimes they will dash at almost anything, and lay hold with such right good will that it is almost impossible to miss them; but these chances do not often occur. Nowadays they are getting so very cautious and cunning, especially where constantly fished for, their education has been complete and thorough, so that any sort of a glaring deception will not work satisfactorily for the angler, at any rate. I have used some brilliant spinners, such as the Francis and the Pennell flights, that will spin a bait in a most attractive-looking manner; but, somewhat or other, results do not point them out as being the best that can be used.

In spinning for pike in a slow-running river like the Bedfordshire Ouse, or the clear water of some of the Norfolk Broads; or again in the generally bright water of some inland lake that is fed from hillside springs, it is necessary first to mount the bait so that no more of the hooks are visible than can possible be helped; second, use no more of those hooks than are really necessary; third, use them as small as you dare; and, fourth, spin slowly if possible, and see that the bait wobbles and comes through the water in all sorts of curious curves and twists. I once saw a couple of anglers spinning on the river just named; one fancied himself as an expert of the first water, the other was a novice pure and simple. "Look at that now, my boy," says the expert as he swung his brilliantly-mounted bait right across the river, and spun it back close to the surface with great rapidity and in one straight and even line. His companion did look, but could not imitate that cast if he tried for a week. In all probability if a good jack had seen that bait he would have wondered at the curious apparition, and known very well that fish are not naturally in the habit of going across the river in that headlong manner. That angler's companion, the novice, had a very simple flight, on which he mounted a bait in a very rough and ready manner. He was constantly getting into difficulties with his reel and line in throwing out, so that the

bait would nearly sink to the bottom before he got all
straight; the bait itself would sink and draw, wobble and
twist, but—and here is where our expert wondered—this
novice caught the fish. Why? Because by accident he
had without knowing it imitated the actions of a bait in
difficulties.

The very best flight that I ever used in slow-running
waters was the simple two-treble flight of the Trent men,
and the size of hooks No. 5 or 4 Redditch scale, plenty
large enough. These two hooks are whipped nearly close
together, so that there is not more than a quarter of an inch
of gimp between the end of the shank of the bottom hook
and the bends of the top treble. When the water is very
bright and clear No. 5 hooks will be the best, and they will
be all the better by being dressed on, say, five inches only
of ooo copper gimp (the finest size); a single strand of
strong stained salmon gut can be joined to that little
bit of gimp by two neatly, but strongly, whipped loops;

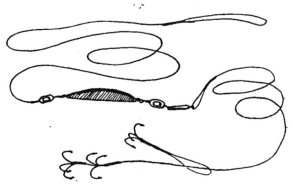

FIG. 11. THE "TRENT OTTER'S" FLIGHT AND TRACE.

one good long single strand will do, so that the flight proper, gimp and gut, is about 16in. in length. For this clear
water spinning a trace of one and a half yards in length of
strong single salmon gut is best, with a drop-lead and buckle
swivel on the end, and also one or two more swivels in it
above the lead. When the water is clouded or charged in

any way with colour it does not matter so much about using
gut, gimp will do then very well.

The best natural baits for spinning are small dace, say
of about five inches long; large bleak, or whitlings as they
are known on the Trent, and toughened sprats; these last
two are rather tender and require mounting on the hooks
in a very careful manner; but all three of them are splendid bright and glittering spinning baits to use in a clouded
water. Small roach, gudgeon, or the tail-end of an eel are
also pretty fair spinning baits, the two latter the most useful perhaps when the water is very clear. In using small
dace or roach I suppose I need not say that the fresher they
are the better; indeed, I fancy it is the best if possible to
carry them down to the riverside in a bait can alive, and
knock them on the head before using, and use them fresh
and bleeding. In baiting this two-hook flight that I have
just described, you detach the hook part of the tackle from
the buckle swivel of the trace, and with the aid of the
baiting needle pass the loop in at the vent of the bait, and
bring it out of the mouth, pulling it through till the shank
of the top treble is in the vent of the bait; you then stick one
hook of the end treble in the root of the tail about the centre,
or perhaps a little nearer the back. This causes the bait,
when the hooks are pulled tight, to bend slightly downwards and sideways, giving it that attractive wobbling spin
that I have found so deadly. This tackle, threaded through
the bait like that, is very neat, and does not show the
small hooks anything like so plainly as the ordinary side-
hooked flight does. I found after a very long and careful
trial of this flight in quiet, or nearly quiet, waters that with
the two trebles being close together and near the tail-end
of bait, it was possible to miss your fish if the pike seized
it by the head end. So to counteract this somewhat I made
a small addition in the shape of another very small treble,
which is dressed or firmly whipped on a loop of fine gimp
one inch in length from the end of the shank. After the
bait is put on as already described, this small looped treble
is dropped over the gut or gimp of the flight, and brought
down to the nose of the bait, and one of the hooks is then
stuck in the side towards the back, on the same side of the

bait as the tail-end hook is, as far beyond the gill covers as the small loop will allow it to go. This is a valuable addition to that tackle; since I adopted it I have hooked a fair percentage of my pike on that top loose treble. I once saw an illustration of a Nottingham spinning flight, and the method there said to be adopted by the Trent men in mounting a bait on that tackle. The two treble hooks were there, but rather further apart than usual, and instead of the gimp being threaded completely through the bait from the vent to the nose, the two hooks were simply stuck in the side about middle way, and the loop of the gimp passed under the gill covers and out at the mouth. For years I fished the Trent in company with some of the very best men who lived on its banks, and I never once saw a bait mounted in that manner; indeed, I greatly question if one could be used there with any chance of success. Heavy currents are very prevalent in that river, and pretty long casting has also to be the order of the day in a very many places. The bait would soon be thrown loose or wear away from the hooks by the action of the current, and very soon be hanging by only the little bit of gimp under the gill covers. It hardly mattered how many or how few hooks were used on a Trent flight, the main principle of mounting was alike in nearly every case, the gimp being threaded through the centre of the bait and the hook or hooks close to the tail. Of course I saw strangers at times using different kinds of flights, sometimes having one treble, sometimes two, and sometimes three trebles, and a lip hook fixed outside the bait; but the old-experienced anglers, who had had a lifetime's experience, always considered the gimp should go through the centre of the bait to have the best results. An old saw runs, that "the proof of the pudding is in the eating," and my strong recommendation of this tackle is based very much on the same lines. In the first place I have done well with it in all sorts and conditions of waters, down the heavy streams of the Trent, on the deep and sluggish waters of the Ouse, across the weedy shallows of the same river, and among the reedy fastnesses of broads, lakes, and backwaters.

During the season 1889-90 I was out on public waters

twenty different days, and successfully landed on that flight 79 sizeable jack, to say nothing of the scores put back that were undersized. That was my best season as far as pike fishing was concerned, and the result fully confirmed. my previous good opinion of the flight. In the second place, the tackle is cheap, and as these pages are written more particularly in the interest of the working man, I don't feel justified in recommending an expensive flight or spinner, when one costing about sixpence is as much or even more effective. In spinning over places when the water is shallow and weedy, and very little, if any, stream at all is running, it will be necessary to spin rather near the surface and a little quicker than in waters deeper and clearer from weeds. It is not the correct thing to spin your bait home like lightning under any circumstances, if it can anyhow be avoided. In a deep and sluggish water which is comparatively speaking free from weeds and obstructions, let it sink deep down until you think it nearly touches the bottom, and keep moving your rod point at intervals during the process of winding the bait home from right to left, and back again ; and then again let the rod point drop towards the water, raising it again after a few seconds, all the time winding home slowly. These movements of the rod, and varying the pace of the bait, all have a tendency to cause that bait to come through the water in a series of curious curves, dives, and twists, which in my opinion is the main source of attraction. A wobbling bait with an uneven spin I have proved over and over again to be far more deadly than a bait spun home in one long, straight, and glittering line. Just before the bait reaches the end of its journey, that is, within two or three yards from where you stand, before you lift it out for a fresh cast, it will be as well to lower the rod point to nearly the surface of the water, and fish the place clean out, if you anyhow can ; that is, let the bait come as close as possible to the bank on which you stand. Sometimes a good jack will follow the bait from right across the river and take it close under your feet. He probably thought it was trying to escape from him by diving under the bank, whereas if the bait had been lifted out when at full length of the rod, he would have turned tail

F

and retreated back again. I have seen this done more than
once. If you see the jack following the bait with his nose .
nearly against it, as I have done lots of times, and you stop
spinning for a moment and let the bait sink a trifle, in six
cases out of ten Mr. Pike will dive after it in a hurry and
lay fiercely hold.   But in all these proceedings you must
keep a cool head and a steady eye, and be ready to tighten
on him at any moment; don't get flurried like a friend of
mine once did when throwing his first spinning bait. A
good jack came at the bait in deadly earnest, when it was
close to the surface, and within half a dozen yards of the
angler. This sudden onslaught so frightened our fisherman that he dropped the rod and sprang backwards in
alarm, thus losing his first run. I admit that it is a bit
startling to a beginner, the sudden rush of a fair-sized pike,
when you are thinking of lifting the bait out for a fresh
cast, is enough to unnerve the inexperienced in such matters, but if he takes it deep down out of sight, the first experience is not so startling.

If the place you spin over is choked with weeds, that is,
growing in a dense mass everywhere, with only a few spots
where there is six inches of clear water above those weeds,
and here and there a rather deeper opening, don't miss it.
Very often the best jack lie lurking among those weeds, but
keep the bait near the surface, above the weeds, and also
work it well in the clear runs between the beds. When you
first begin to fish a likely-looking stretch of water, it is not
the correct thing to throw your bait right out to the furthest
extent of your cast; but just toss it into the nearest opening
at first, and gradually work further away in every direction,
until you cover the entire distance you can comfortably
reach; searching the nearest water first should always be
strictly attended to. Any sort of water, provided it is fairly
clear, can be spun over. I once heard an old angler say
that spinning proper could only be done in weir pools and
streams, and down the faster currents of a running river;
but this is all nonsense. Ponds, lakes, railway cuttings,
meres, broads, or anywhere else, provided pike live in it,
can be successfully operated on if a clear opening can be
found. In casting it is a general thing to throw the bait

across and down stream, if there is any stream, and draw
it back against the current searching all the possible water
well over. I have found after searching the water by that
plan to have had a slice of luck by throwing the bait up
stream and drawing it down the same direction as the current is running. Many a good fish have I picked up by
this plan, after having searched all the water by the ortho-
dox down-stream cast. I have sometimes fancied that it
was because the bait looked more natural going down
stream.

Another flight that was a particular favourite with one or
two of my friends was constructed on the same lines as the
flight I described a little while ago, except the tail-end hook,
which instead of being a treble was a large single hook some
three-quarters of an inch wide in the bend with a shank
fully an inch long. Immediately at the end of this shank
a small treble, about a No. 6, was firmly whipped to the
same gimp, and the loose looped treble completed the
tackle. This flight is baited the same as the other, with
the gimp run through the body from the vent to the mouth,
the single hook at the end being stuck firmly into the solid
flesh near the tail in such a manner that the tail itself bent
slightly towards the right hand, and a full quarter inch or
more of the point and barb of the hook protruding free.
One old spinner of long and wide experience would have it
that this tackle was a slight improvement on my favourite,
one reason being that the large hook at the end buried, or
nearly so, in the tail of the bait gave it a more brilliant
spin ; and another reason was the treble hooks being a
shade smaller, and also the tail-end hook being nearly hid
gave the tackle a neater appearance, and nothing much
except the bait visible to the keen eyes of the jack. I had
to admit on looking at the two flights when baited that this
was so ; but it had one drawback, it was not such a safe-
hooking tackle as mine. I very seldom lost one when
hooked ; he had several mishaps in this direction. I simply
laid the difference to be his use of too small trebles. There
are several more flights and tackles in use for spinning a
dead bait; but I don't propose to look at the merits or
demerits of any of them here. I have given a full descrip-

tion of how I consider a bait should be spun, and also the best style of mounting that bait to give the best results. When a whole host of tackles are recommended and described, it makes a book look, in my idea, more like a manufacturer's catalogue than a practical guide to the sport.

And now I must give a few words as to the best condition of the water to expect sport in. Some little time ago I mentioned the very best season's jack spinning I ever had, and turning to my note-book to find out to what cause I attribute the sport there alluded to, I find on a careful perusal that nearly the whole of the time the water was clouded, and the best fish and best days were when it reads: " Water very much clouded." When I say very much clouded, I don't mean a tearing pea-soup flood, nor anything like that, but a fair colour in which the bait is nicely visible when sunk a foot below the surface, and when sunk a couple of feet or so it can still be seen, but looks to be in a decided haze. This was the condition of the water when I got my best bags. Very fair sport indeed was had occasionally when the bait could be seen when sunk three feet below the surface. Anything brighter than this was not conducive to great success. Some time ago I read an article that was published in one of the angling journals, in which the writer boldly declared that the water could not be too clear for spinning, especially spinning with a spoon. My experience is exactly opposite. I have thrown a spinning bait thousands of casts in all sorts and conditions of waters, and even when a natural bait was used success was all the greater when the water was clouded, and this was even more to be noted when spinning with a spoon. In 1892 I find on reference to my note-book that the water in the River Ouse had been for several weeks exceedingly low and clear, and no sport to speak about. Then came some heavy rain, and a flush of water came down the river. On one afternoon when the water rose at least two feet during the time I was fishing, and was " heavily charged with colour," as my note-book has it, I ran no less than 18 pike, some of them very good ones indeed, in not more than one and a half miles of water. The same water, bear in mind, that I had thrown over a dozen times previously during its extreme brightness with scarcely any success; in fact, a careful perusal of my note-book for several seasons confirms this. When the water was very clear and bright—when every hook is plainly visible halfway across the river to both fish and fisherman, it is very little good throwing a bait. I have tried under these conditions all sorts of dodges, using a single gut trace with the very smallest hooks dressed on ooo copper gimp, and only four or five inches of this, just where the pike's teeth are likely to be if he takes hold; and for bait a four-inch glittering bleak. I have stirred the fish certainly—fair sized ones I mean—and seen them follow it, and tried everything I knew to make them take hold, but no, they appeared to me to be a deal too crafty to take a bait when even that fine tackle was so plainly exposed. Small ones of a pound, or even less under these conditions, are apt to be a nuisance; they will persist in taking the bait when their elders consider that bait is to be avoided at any cost. I have been forced to put extra bright water as one of the conditions not very conducive to sport when spinning. A few odd small ones may be got, with here and there at long intervals a fair sized one; but that is about all. Of course, I am now alluding to public rivers that are pretty well spun over nearly every day. A good private water that is not so hunted to death, especially if it is a clear-water lake, is a different thing; it hardly matters what sort of tackle is used, or what sort of baits, the only condition being whether the fish are on the feed or dead off.

In spinning over public well-fished waters, when the streams have run down very sluggish and they are gin-bright, a gudgeon is as good a bait as can be tried, and this should be mounted on very small hooks with a trace of pale blue stained salmon gut. An eel-tail mounted on a large single hook, with a bit of lead round the shank is also another very good clear-water spinning bait. The looped side treble, as recommended for spinning a dace, will also be a valuable addition to the eel-tail bait. In a clouded water the two best baits to use are bleak and sprats, next to these come dace, while roach or any other small fish can be tried if nothing else is forthcoming. In a river or lake where the jack run very large and the water is at all coloured,

it is not advisable by any means to use too fine tackle for
spinning, No. o size copper gimp being plenty fine enough,
while if the water is clear perhaps it will be better to have
the last two feet of the tackle a size, or even two sizes,
finer gimp.   In spinning for jack on a large lake or broad,
where the water is deep and the fish very sluggish, and
moreover where you are as likely to get hold of a twenty-
pounder as a three, it is not a bit of good spinning near the
surface, those large and lazy jack are not going to be at the
trouble or rising all that distance.   If the water is free from
sunken trees or other large obstructions, you must use a
heavier lead and larger bait, and let it sink deep down,
spinning it home very slowly, and chance hooking on to a
stray weed bed now and again.   For this sort of spinning
it will be as well to have a stronger and heavier set of
tackle, with hooks of a fair good size, say No. 1's, at the very
least, so that a 5 or 6 oz. dace or roach can be mounted
comfortably on them.   It is the only way to get the large
ones spinning that live deep down in the sluggish depths of
quiet deep water.   Of course they can be got at by live-
baiting with a paternoster tackle, but just now, remember,
I am treating of spinning with a dead bait.   On the
other hand, in spinning over a canal or small stream, or
even a backwater, where a five-pound fish is a rarity not
often met with, and the fishermen themselves are nearly as
numerous as the fish, the tackle can scarcely be too fine nor
the bait too neatly mounted; five inches of the best ooo
copper gimp on which the hooks are dressed, then 18in. of
strong single barbel gut, then the drop-lead and two swivels,
and finally two more feet of very strong single gut.   This is
about the best arrangement that can be tried under the
circumstances just alluded to, and for bait an ounce dace or
a four-inch sprat.   In spinning over well-fished water when
it has run down very clear, sometimes you stir a fish, you
see a good jack move, probably only just notice a swirl
under the water, Mr. Jack came and went again, refusing the
bait.   It is a good plan to keep pegging away for ten
minutes or more over the same place with the same bait,
although you feel that he does not mean to have it; but I
believe you are aggravating the fish, and after a time slip

the bait off you are using and substitute another totally
different in shape and colour, and throw again; the chances
are that he will take it with a savage grab the first time.
Some people tell us that if a pike stirs to a spinning bait
and refuses it, it is best to give him an hour's rest and then
try again. My advice is to keep throwing over him, a dozen
or even a score of times, until he probably knows every
outline of that bait, and then put on something else of a
different shape and colour, and very often success will crown
this little dodge. I remember once in particular the club
I belonged to fishing a pike spinning match one afternoon.
One of the competitors, who was fishing a cunning corner
of the river, told me that he had stirred a good fish nearly
an hour previously, and although he had stuck to it well, not
another move did he see. He was spinning with a bright
and glittering dace. He told me that as he was off to another place I might have a go at that fish if I liked, and I
fancied there was a sort of sarcasm in his tone. However,
I took off my natural dace that I had been using, and put
on an old dull-coloured wobbling spoon, and got him the
first cast; and it turned out to be the first prize fish. This
is only one instance out of several in my long experience
when a change of bait has resulted in success. When a
fish is just slightly hooked, and then after a few seconds'
play lost, it is not much use in a general way to keep
throwing over him; give him an hour's rest if you anyhow
can before trying again. Some odd times he will come
again instantly; indeed, I have had one or two fish that have
been hooked and lost three times in less than ten minutes,
and then got him the very next cast. It is not often, however, that they are so very accommodating as this. If, after
losing one, you find he does not come again in two or three
casts, you can safely leave him to settle down for an hour
or so.

And now just a word or two on a very vexed question,
and that is, should a pike be sharply struck when hooked
on a spinning tackle? My decided opinion is—no, certainly.
I believe that more pike are lost when hooked by striking
too heavily, than if you don't strike at all. A pike generally
collars the bait when it is revolving through the water. If

you strike at once and sharply, the chances are that you will snatch bait and hooks out of his mouth. He may lay hold in such a manner that scarcely any of the hooks are in a position to bury themselves in his jaws, and a sudden stroke may pull the lot away after two or three seconds' play, whereas if you waited for a second, holding tight until the fish turned, the hooks have a better chance to bury themselves below the barb. When I am spinning a bait home and feel a sudden check deep below the surface I keep on winding until a strong pull in the opposite direction tells me that a fish is going off, I never slaken for a moment if anyhow possible, but keep my finger tightly pressed on the edge of reel and let him drag strongly for every foot of line he takes out. There is no necessity to let a pike run away with a lot of line if you can in any way prevent it. Of course if it is a very large one the case is a bit different, but moderate sized jack should be stopped before they have a chance to run you into difficulties among the weeds. I always play a fish heavily from the very first, and find this quite sufficient to hook them securely without striking sharply at all. Of course you know thereabouts what your line and tackle will stand, but it is folly to allow a five or six pounder to run right across the river and all over the place. I have killed, or at least got, eight-pound pike out of the water in three minutes after being hooked; but as an old friend put it, I always did take energetic measures with my pike when hooked. I did not believe in letting them run headlong into a bunch of weeds or round an old post or two if a little persuasion could keep them out; but the extent of this persuasion would have to be governed by the nature of the stream, the size of the fish, and the fineness or otherwise of the tackle.

It is not advisable under any circumstances when using spinning tackle to strike suddenly and heavily. The fish might be a heavy one, and the jerk might result in disaster to the line or tackle. In waters that are nearly choked up with weeds, where it is necessary to spin the bait near to the surface, it is far the best to give a hooked fish no more law than can be helped; keep a tight line on him, and get him to shore as quickly as possible. You might as well lose

him one way as another, if he bolts right under the weeds,
why he is as good as lost; but if you can keep him near the
surface the chances of getting him out are good. If you
really cannot do this owing to the fish being a large one,
you will have to chance it and let him go and trust to luck
to land him. In spinning over deep waters, or indeed any
waters, and a hooked jack suddenly, as it were, stands on
his tail with his upper part straight above the surface, opens
his jaws and gills wide, and shakes his head like a savage
dog, you stand a very good chance of losing that fish; but
don't be flurried, keep the line tight; if you let the line go
very slack he will probably shake the hooks out. A tight
line is the only way to save that fish if it can anyhow be
saved.   A hard and fast line cannot be set down as to how
a pike should be played. The angler should consider the
circustances attached to each individual place, and lay his
plans accordingly. I certainly have found it the best to
take prompt measures if the cast was in a dangerous place,
and trust to having a broken tackle. And, finally, while I
am on with the subject of playing and landing a pike, I
may say that if a large landing-net is used don't on any account try to use it until the hooked fish is well within reach.
And then use it as promptly and quickly as possible; get it
well under him and lift him speedily out before he has time
to jump out again. In using a spinning tackle the hooks are
liable to catch in the net before you get the fish fairly in
as well, and if this happens you will be landed in a sweet
little difficulty, and in all probability lose the fish. I found
the best plan was to hold the pike's head above the surface,
run the net up behind him, and scoop him out at once. In
some waters it is a frequent occurrence for hooked pike to
leap a couple of feet or even more into the air; when
this happens, if you keep putting a heavy drag on the line
you are liable to part company at once. The best plan is
to instantly, as soon as he jumps, lower the rod point, and
very slightly ease the pressure of the finger on the edge of
the reel, so that he could have a yard of line if necessary,
taking care, however, that the line is by no means slack;
the pressure should always be tight enough to prevent the
reel from paying out more loose line than is required.

Nothing is more fatal when playing a hooked fish than to have some loose line hanging about the reel handles. Every yard of line that I allowed a pike to take out had to be worked for by the fish.

The best months for spinning are September, October, and November. December is fairly good, but the pike then are getting fat and lazy, seeking the deepest and quietest holes as a general thing. There is nothing in law to prevent spinning for pike in public waters as soon as the season opens in June, unless a fishery board, for the district extends the close time. I most certainly do consider that June and July should be observed as a close time by every pike fisherman; while even in August those fish are by no means in condition. During the early part of the season pike are found on the weedy shallows of a quiet river, being also very partial to a streamy place that flows over a gravelly bottom, runs in the vicinity of flags, reed beds, water lilies, and bunches of weeds are also affected by them, while good ones are often deep in the fastnesses of the reed beds themselves. Quiet corners away from the main current, eddies at the tail of an island, behind some sunken trees and bushes; in fact, in a quiet pikey river there is no telling where the jack are and where they are not. All likely or even unlikely places should be well tried, especially during September and October. Later on, towards Christmas time, especially if the weather has been very cold, deeper holes close under the cover of huge banks of weeds would be more likely to shelter the fish. At this time of the year the spinning bait should be sunk deep down and spun very slowly home. In rapidly flowing rivers like the Trent, pike, during the early part of the season, love the eddies that curl round and round from the tail of a weir, or on the shallows away from the main current in quiet corners and lay-byes, or down those long stretches of the river where the water flows much quieter than it does in the majority of places. It is difficult to tell exactly where pike are to be found and where not found during the early part of the season; but if there is a portion of the river that is quiet, weedy, and free from navigation, that is the very place to expect them in. Later on they retire to the deeper and quieter waters, or else seek the pools and backwaters that have outlets or inlets to or from the river.

In spinning for pike it is necessary to have a drop-lead to the trace. By a drop-lead I mean one that hangs below the line, so that it cannot turn over and over in the water. If the lead turns round and round the line will kink up badly. There are several leads that have been specially made for this purpose, one of the best known having a spiral groove running round it. The great merit of this lead lies in the fact that it can be put on the trace exactly where best required for the particular place spun over; also that it can be bent to form the drop to nearly any degree, and that it can be taken off the trace without undoing any part of the tackle, and a lighter or heavier substituted as the particular case requires. My own lead that I have successfully used for a number of years now, is made and mounted on a thin brass wire with a swivel at each end of it. Traces should have at least two swivels in them, and these swivels should be slightly oiled from time to time, as it won't do for them to stick fast during the process of spinning. I give an illustration here of my own particular flight and trace, showing the extra side treble. This trace can be either gut or gimp, according to fancy; but in either case I find the best results are arrived at by having the trace in that particular shape. Sixteen inches is a good distance to have the lead from the bait, and about 30in. of gimp or gut between the lead and the silk running line. Speaking about the spinning line having a tendency to kink, I may say that it is a mistake to have too many swivels in the trace above the lead. I have seen as many as three, or even four, swivels in the trace, and yet the line kinked up worse than if no swivels at all had been used. I found it the best to have two swivels only in the trace, one of them immediately above the lead, and the other just below it. The very thing that some spinners thought would cure a badly kinking line, viz., putting an extra swivel or two in, only served to make the complaint worse.

Years ago we used to sigh for a good preservative, so that baits for spinning could be had when it was impossible to get them in the ordinary way. It used to generally happen

that when we did not want any baits we could catch any
amount of them, and when they were wanted badly not one
could be procured. We tried salting them, putting them
in glycerine, using spirits of wine, and trying a dozen other
dodges, but none of them was a howling success. Of course,
as I have said elsewhere, I preferred them fresh and bleeding if they could be got, but still a good preservative was a
thing badly wanted. Formalin is the latest, and I am
bound to say by experience far the best that has yet been
tried. This mixture has two great merits, it is cheap and
remarkably easy in its application. Experiments have shown
that even the very smallest quantity of formalin among a
quantity of clean water is sufficient to preserve small fish.
A teaspoonful of it to a quart of water is quite ample for
any ordinary purpose. The small fish—sprats are as good
as anything—should be put in a wide-necked bottle, or a
stoppered pickle jar, care being taken that not too many are
put in each bottle, and then filled up with the diluted mixture just named, corked or otherwise fastened securely down.
Sometimes the baits after being in the mixture for a time
turn dirty and look very disagreeable. If this happens the
best plan is to remove the cork, pour away the liquid, wash
the baits well in cold water, rinse out the bottle, put back
the baits, and fill up with a fresh lot of the mixture, only
this time made weaker than before, say a proportion of only
one teaspoonful of the formalin to three pints of water.
One in forty is a strong proposition; one in sixty will do
very well; while even one part to a hundred parts of water
will preserve sprats if they are for immediate use. I might
say that formalin is a poison, but when mixed with water
is harmless. It is a liquid itself and colourless. I don't
advise anyone to mix up more at once than he requires for
the baits he just then wishes to preserve. I trust I have
made this perfectly plain. The formalin itself is a poison,
and should be kept under lock and key away from children.
When mixed with water in its right proportions it is harmless. A teaspoonful to a quart of water is the proportion
to use. Sprats especially, treated like this, are considerably
toughened, and will keep for a long time. I have some now
before me as I write that have been in the bottles eighteen

months, and look as fresh and bright as when first put in; but the angler must remember if he wants them to last for a long time that he must cork and seal them down secure and air-tight if he uses an ordinary wide-necked bottle. A lever-stoppered bottle with a band of expanding indiarubber round the stopper is, however, far the best vessel to employ. I might also add that the small fish that are wanted for preservation, such as sprats, bleak, dace, minnows, stone loach, very small roach, and the tail-end of eels should be put in the preservative when perfectly fresh; on no account should stale ones be used; reject all that are tainted in the slightest, they must be perfectly fresh. I might also add that formalin is sold by The Formalin Co., Ltd.," 10, St. Mary's-at-Hill, London, E.C., at 2s. 6d. per bottle; but most of the tackle dealers now sell the preserved baits in lever-stoppered bottles at ninepence to a shilling per bottle.

In closing this chapter on spinning, I find on looking over my notes that I forgot to mention a very cheap and effective spinning lead that some of my friends on the Trent used years ago. It was simply a piece of sheet lead cut in an oval shape, about one and a half inches long, three-quarters of an inch wide, and one-sixteenth or so of an inch thick. This lead is bent lengthways down the centre, lapped across the trace in its proper place, and pinched tight. This lead can very easily be taken off or put on the line anywhere where wanted, and by being cut in an oval shape and bent in the centre hangs below the line and forms a wonderfully effective drop-lead for spinning. For all other spinning tackles and contrivances for working a dead bait, I must refer the reader to tackle dealers' illustrated catalogues. I have given what I consider to be the best general principles to adopt.

CHAPTER V.

THE PIKE *(continued)*.

SPINNING WITH AN ARTIFICIAL.

Artificial baits—What shape and colour is likely to have the best results—A seeming contradiction—Three typical artificials—How to spin an artificial—Best time, water, and places to try artificials—Wind and weather—Ice in the rings of the rod

Artificial baits for spinning for pike are now made in almost an endless and bewildering variety, and all sorts of material are used in their manufacture, brass, copper, nickel, German silver, aluminium, indiarubber, composition of various kinds, silk, natural skins of fishes, and even bunches of peacock's feathers and silver tinsel, so tied together till the lure looks like a huge humming bird when thrown on the water. Some of these artificials, like the famous "Clipper," for instance, are so constructed that a light breeze is quite sufficient to set them spinning round and round with great rapidity, and when drawn through the water looks like one even and glittering line of silver. This is a famous bait to use when the water is slightly clouded with colour. When the streams have run down very low, and the water is so bright that you can see the bottom very plainly, it is very little good throwing a bright silver-like artificial, or, indeed, for the matter of that, an artificial of any kind, unless it is a soft indiarubber bait of a very dull colour, a good deal after the pattern of the "Jubilee," I think it was called, and even this should be mounted on very fine grey-coloured gimp with hooks small and not much exposed. Almost any artificial, no matter what its name or shape will kill pike some odd times when the conditions are favourable; but tastes seem to vary in different waters. Some waters I have fished in the pike must have a bait that is painted a brilliant red inside with a huge tassel of scarlet wool depending from the far end hook. Others, again, in other waters won't look at one like that, but must have a plain dull-coloured article like the wagtail to tempt them. Some places the pike seem to prefer a small and glittering bait with a very even and rapid spin, a good deal like " Geen's Minnow," while others will have none of it, preferring a wobbling spoon. When we take into consideration all these things it is a very difficult task to determine which bait is likely to be the most useful under all conditions, and as a working man angler cannot afford or does not want to be troubled with one-tenth of the artificials that come under his notice, he would like to know which shape out of the whole lot is most likely to do him the best service. Personally I prefer a good plain spoon; this bait is one of the oldest artificials, and in my opinion still equal to anything or everything that has yet been invented. Pike have been killed on a spoon bait in all British waters where pike are to be found—down-streams like the Trent, or on quieter waters like the Bedfordshire Ouse and the Norfolk Broads. I have an old spoon now in my possession that has killed numbers of fine jack. One season, on reference to my note-book, I found I got no less than 40 with it, many of them reaching a very respectable size, and it is only a plain spoon, gold colour on the outside and bright silver within, with a narrow red line running down the centre on the inside. Some lucky angler on a certain occasion, when everything was in his favour, might be using any one of the numerous artificials that are made, and get a catch that his wildest dreams never thought about before, and straightway write to the sporting papers about his wonderful discovery of the finest artificial that ever was made, whereas he might have been using something else at the time totally different in shape and colour, and had the same luck on that. He might use the same bait a dozen times afterwards and not meet with anything like such success again. On one occasion I got 40lb. of jack during a single afternoon on my old spoon bait, but the weather and the water was in an extremely favourable condition, and the fish fairly on the rampage; and once the Clipper accounted for nine good fish in one day; but I should not like to say by any means that just because on those occasions I was lucky enough to get the fish that those baits will kill any time and under any conditions. It is only by a most careful trial during a number of seasons, and a most careful record of fish caught that a decision affecting this point can be arrived at. One season on the Trent there was not another bait that could touch " Bink's Jubilee" spinner as an artificial. This is a soft rubber bait, if my memory is to be trusted, while since that time I cannot hear that it has once met with more than ordinary success. A friend of mine who occasionally fishes in the big Irish loughs tells me that one day the pike of those waters seem to prefer a large Devon minnow of a dull brown or blue colour, while the next a bright silver Clipper with a red tassel at the tail seemed to have the greatest attraction; and still again, the very next day they would not run at either, but would take a huge wobbling spoon. Looking at my own practical experience I am forced to the conclusion that a good plain spoon of some two and a half inches in length, coloured either copper or gold on the outside, bright silver inside, with a red line down the centre (this line, by the way, can be painted on with a drop of the varnish mentioned elsewhere, mixed with a pinch of vermillion, and applied with a small camel-hair brush) is the best artificial that can yet be employed, even if it is somewhat old-fashioned. It must be 35 years since I saw a spoon bait used for the first time down a Lincolnshire canal, and as two or three fair good jack were taken on it on that occasion, I thought it a most wonderful bait. And so it is with most amateur pike spinners; just because a certain artificial on one occasion killed a good bag of fish, they needs must swear by that particular bait for ever afterwards. But some of the most curious pike spinning experiences I have ever had have been made up of contradictions pure and simple. One day the jack down a certain stretch of water would come at a bait of one particular shape and colour only, utterly ignoring anything else I happened to try; while the next day that bait itself was left alone and one of the rejected ones of the previous day would prove successful. In the face of all these diffi-

-culties and contradictions, it is a hopeless task, in fact I
have had far too long a practical experience in pike fishing
-on various waters to attempt to recommend any one particular artificial as the very best that can be employed. As I
said a little while ago, if I have a preference for any one,
that one is an ordinary spoon; but when a pike spinner has
killed over two hundred jack during his career on spoon
baits in well-fished public waters, he is apt to speak feel-
ingly. Here are three typical baits now before me that re-
present extremes in artificials. First there is an old wobbling spoon, that twists, curves, dives, and spins with a curious
erratic movement, especially in still, or nearly still, water;
second, there is the Clipper, a most brilliant silvery fish
shaped bait with a scarlet tassel that spins extremely rapid
and in one straight line; third, there is the Wagtail, a most
curious bait made out of a thin and narrow, or rather two
narrow strips of soft indiarubber, of a dull colour, which,
when drawn through the water, seems to throb and heave
like something alive and breathing. These are totally
opposed to one another as far as shape, colour, and spinning powers are concerned, and yet I should say under certain conditions they all would meet with occasional sport.
There are also dozens more artificials that come up in some
particular way or other to those just named, which might
be equally successful. It is no use pinning your faith on
any one of them. Sometimes after an unsuccessful day
with an artificial you might say, " Now, if I had had such
and such a bait I might have got hold of one or two," when
in all probability, no matter what you used, the result might
have been the same. It depends more upon two things
than the shape and colour of the artificial. First, the condition of the water, and, second, whether the pike are on the
feed or not. Putting it broadly then, I should say that if
your tackle case contained three different types of artificials
that are opposed to each other in shape, colour, and spinning powers, I care not under what name they are known,
nor yet who is the manufacturer of them, the chances are
that one or the other of them would some time during the
day attract the attention, and so arouse the curiosity of a
pike that he would throw prudence to the winds and seize

G

hold, although the water might be as clear as gin, and everything unfavourable for the sport.   It is only by acting
dodges like the one I gave in the previous chapter, that is
after throwing some considerable time over a place that you
know holds a good jack, without success, or at most which
only moves him, with one kind of artificial, slip another
one on as much opposed to the one you have been using
as you have got, and he may come the very next throw.
You can never tell your luck; you can only keep pegging
away, chopping and changing about, first one artificial and
then another, sometimes spinning quickly then again more
slowly; sometimes deep down in the water, and then again
nearer the surface.   It is only by this that a jack will repose
in the bag at close of day, that is, bear in mind, when the
water is extremely clear and everything unfavourable, remem-
bering always what a well-known angler once said when
writing to one of the angling journals: "That you cannot
expect to catch many fish if your rod is all the time reared
up against a tree."   I cannot hold with the remarks that
the writer I previously quoted used in one of his articles,
that the water could not be too clear for spinning with an
artificial, especially a spoon.   It appeared to me to be a
necessity that in certain waters, particularly in well-fished
public rivers, that a certain amount of colour should be in
the water; but see what I say on this subject in the previous
chapter on spinning with a dead bait.   Those remarks hold
good in discussing the use of an artificial.
    In rivers like the Trent, that are subject after heavy rains
to sudden and thick water floods, that come tearing down
with terrific force, it is very little good to throw an artificial of any kind while the water is in that state, rather
wait a little until it has somewhat fined down; in fact so
much that when your bait is sunk two or three feet down
below the surface you can see it gleam, as it were, in a
haze.   Try then all the quieter corners and lay-byes, letting
it sink deep down and spinning home no faster than is
really necessary.   Taking it all round the Trent fishes very
well indeed when it is moderately clear, that is as far as
pike spinning is concerned; but I should suppose this is
because it is a very wide river with a good volume of water
generally running.

In quieter waters like the Ouse, the Witham, and similar
streams, I found it the best for spinning when the water
was on the rise, and once or twice I have had very good
bags when it has been too thick to see the spoon when sunk
a couple of feet below the surface. During the late summer and early autumn, when the water is very clear, almost
the only chance you have to pick up a fish by spinning an
artificial is just after sunset, immediately before the dusk of
evening creeps down on you. I have had some of my very
best fish under these circumstances. A splendid place to
try an artificial is in the rough and broken water at the
foot of a weir, particularly if large stones and sunken trees
break the force of the stream and form eddies behind. If
the frothing waters keep churning round and round, and
you hardly think there is room to get a spinning bait in,
never mind, have a try, there might be a specimen lurking
under the shadow of those big stones. I am very fond of
spinning in all those streams and eddies that curl round and
round from the foot of a weir. The same trace and drop-
lead that I recommend for spinning a natural bait will do
for an artificial, only when water is clouded, weeds and obstructions are plentiful, and fish run large, I should use them
rather thicker than ordinary, say No. 1 gimp; but on well-
fished rivers like the Lea and Stort, say, when water is clear,
gut traces and small hooks must be the order of the day.
And now just a word or two on another very vexed question,
and that is what wind and weather are likely to be the best
for sport with a spinning bait, either dead or an artificial?
Some anglers prefer a gale of wind, when the water is rolled
up in miniature waves, caused by the wind chopping or
blowing up-stream. Certainly I have had some sport under
circumstances like that, but then on the other hand I
have had far better luck when not even a wind ripple disturbed the surface of the water. Once in particular, I find
on reference to my note-book, that I had been spinning all
one afternoon when the water was clouded and the wind
blowing just sufficient to ripple and disturb the surface; but
not a touch did I get. Towards evening the wind suddenly
died down, not so much as a move could be seen on the
water, and the rain that had been threatening all day came

down in earnest. Not caring to go home with a blank, I
again tried over a place that I had twice previously thrown
over during the afternoon without success, and within the
next half-hour five fish going 25lb. lay on the bank. I am
forced to admit that several of my best bags have been taken
during a dead calm. I don't think it matters in the slightest
when the water is clouded a little as to whether there is a
good breeze or not. If the water is very clear then the
case is different, a little wind being necessary to hide the
angler's movements and the deception of his line and tackle.
I have taken jack when spinning in all sorts of weather—
when a gale nearly blew me into the river, when a light
chopping wind only just rippled and disturbed the surface,
and also when not a breath of air could be discerned. You
cannot lay down a hard and fast line in this respect, but
speaking generally and broadly I should say, taking all
things into consideration, the whole season through, clear
water and clouded, a little breeze stands the best chance of
sport. As regards the best quarter for the wind to be in, I
don't think it matters very much where it is. A strong east
wind with a touch of frost that will clean drive the roach off
the feed, will sometimes serve to make the pike ravenous.
Wind and weather don't matter very much. One of the
most favourable conditions to find the water in is after a
few frosts have rotted the weeds, then a heavy rain which
causes a rapid rise and sweeps the decayed weeds away and
washes the jack from out their fastnesses into the more
open water. As soon as this flood-water clears away sufficiently to enable the bait to be seen fairly well, then that
most assuredly is the time for getting sport. I have got
jack spinning when the weather has been very warm and
summerlike, and also have got them when the frost has been
so keen that every few minutes I have been obilged to suck
the ice from out the rings of the rod; when a nor'-easter
has been raging; when the rain has been coming down in
dead earnest; and also during a snowstorm. In spinning
during very frosty weather the ice will accumulate in the
rings of the rod and cause considerable trouble and annoy-
ance. Several things have been recommended to counteract
this somewhat, but none of them appear to me to be a per-

manent success. The spinning line is generally an undressed silk, and holds water to some extent, so naturally
freezes. You cannot do better than rub a few drops of
castor oil, applied with a flannel, down the line before starting out on a frosty day. This is the best remedy I know
of, but grinding the line in and out the rings when the latter
are nearly choked up with ice is not one of the best things
to subject a line to. If ice forms in the end ring or any
of the rings for the matter of that, you must suck it out
again and chance the disagreeableness of the task.

CHAPTER VI.

THE PIKE *(continued)*.

The reel, line, and tackle—How to bait a dead gorge—Working the trolling bait—Different methods of dead gorging.

Trolling for pike with a dead gorge bait is a sport that I don't hold with, if the place operated on can anyhow be got at with a spinning bait. All hooked fish, no matter how small, must be killed after swallowing a dead gorge. It is true there is a disgorger made now that will occasionally get up gorge hooks without hurting the fish very much, more particularly live gorge tackle; but the fact that the gimp of a dead gorge is threaded completely through the bait, and also that a lead is cast round the shank of the hooks, prevents the disgorger just named from getting to the points of the hooks on purpose to push them back. But as there are certain waters containing good pike that cannot possibly be got at by any other plan, I must just briefly look at it, but this chapter will be a very short one indeed.

Certain backwaters, pools, railway cuttings, etc., etc., are very often so choked up with weeds that there is scarcely a hole a yard square anywhere all over the surface, and yet good jack are known to be in those waters, the object of a dead gorge being so that when it is moved up and down in a sink and draw movement and a pike swallows it, there are no hooks, no leads, and no float to catch among the weeds and so help him to shake himself free; and if the pike does thread himself in and out among those weeds you stand a chance of getting him out if line and tackle are strong, which they ought to be in dead-gorging, and the weeds

somewhat rotten and tender. I remember once seeing a
very large jack taken by this method, which, when landed,
was so embedded among a huge lump of weeds that it positively could not be seen; weeds and jack together must
have weighed close on a hundredweight. In dead-gorging
among the weeds the rod should be as stiff and as strong
as possible, and the line as strong as you like; in fact, it
cannot be too strong. One of those tanned plaited hemp
ones, No. 1 or 2 size, that is capable of standing a strain of
from thirty to forty pounds, will be plenty good enough for
this purpose, and as a forty or fifty yard length only runs
from two shillings to half-a-crown the price need not be a
serious consideration. I don't recommend a good silk spinning line for this job; if the angler is in the habit of frequently fishing certain waters among the weeds with a dead
gorge it will pay him to have a strong, easy-going, cheap,
wooden reel, and a length of plaited hemp line, and use
them for that purpose only, the price would not exceed five
shillings for both, and as this line is rather sharp and harsh
in its texture it would be likely to saw through a bunch of
dead weeds like a reaping hook when a big jack threaded
his way through. The usual gorge hook is simply a double
hook of the pattern or shape known as a parrot beak,
securely fastened to a short length of stout twisted brass
wire, hook and wire being about five inches long over all; a
piece of lead reaching from nearly the bends of the hooks
to within a couple of inches of the small eye at end of wire,
that is about three inches long and three-eighths of an inch
thick in the centre, tapering slightly towards each end, is
cast on the shank of hook and the brass wire in such a
manner that the whole is stiff and rigid. Joined to the
small eye at end of wire is a length of strong gimp, say from
18in. to 2ft., and this gimp should be fairly strong and in
keeping with the rest of the tackle. A short trace without
any lead on, say about a couple of feet long, with a strong
buckle swivel on the end, completes the troller's outfit.
The lead is inside the bait, so none is required on the trace;
besides you want nothing on the line to catch over or under
the weeds, more than you can possibly help. It would be
all the better if there was not even a swivel; but I con-

sider a swivel a very necessary evil for this work, as without
it the line is liable to kink when wet.

In baiting a gorge hook, the loop of the gimp is put in
the eye of a baiting needle, and the point of this thrust
down the throat of the bait, keeping it as near the backbone
as possible, and as near the centre of the fish as you can,
so that the leaded wire will have a foundation of solid flesh
to rest in, and not be so liable to tear away by contact with
the weeds as it would do if threaded through the intestines
only.   Bring the needle out between the forks of the tail,
and carefully draw the gimp through until the lead and wire
are completely hidden in the bait, with the bends of the
hooks close up to the nose.   Some anglers then tie the tail
with a bit of fine twine or shoemaker's flax to the gimp,
wrapping it round and round, so that there are no inequali-
ties hanging free to catch under the weeds when the bait is
withdrawn from the water.   Other men clip the tail off
altogether with a pair of scissors, but one plan would, I
daresay, be as good as the other.   Now remove the baiting
needle and fasten the loop of the gimp into the buckle
swivel of the trace, join the latter neatly with a good fast
knot to the running line, and all is ready for action.   The
best bait for trolling is a good five-inch dace, a small roach
will do, so will a large gudgeon; but a dace appears to me
to be the best shape for shooting down quickly, besides being tough and lasting on the hooks.

Where trolling with a dead gorge differs in a material
manner from spinning with a dead bait, is the fact that
almost any preserved or pickled fish will do for the latter,
the former must have a bait perfectly fresh.   When a pike
runs at a spinning bait and lays hold, he has no chance, as
a rule, to reject it, whereas if the taste of a dead gorge was
not to his liking, he could drop it at once.   I found that
if a bait was freshly killed, and slipped on the gorge when
bleeding, the chances would be much better than if the bait
was old and stale.   In trolling, the angler selects the
clearest place he can find and draws down a length of line
from between the rings of the rod, and just tosses the bait
towards that opening, at the same time leaving go of the
loop or length of line he holds in one hand.   As soon as

the bait hits the water it will dive down very quickly, the
heavy lead inside it causing this.   Always keep a tight line;
don't have any slack hanging loose if you can possibly help
it.   As soon as the bait begins to dive downwards lower the
point of the rod until you think the bait has gone far enough,
and then raise the point slowly until it again comes near the
surface, then drop the rod again quickly so as to cause
the bait to again shoot downwards towards the bottom, repeating this a few times until the bait works too near the
weeds; then withdraw it as well as you can, clear off what
stray weeds may be sticking to the hooks, and make a fresh
cast.   If the water is very much choked up with weeds, you
cannot very well work a gorge bait in a small opening beyond
the reach of your rod; if you can reach the place with your
rod point it will be all the better.   I have known before now
a long 18-foot bamboo, stiff and strong, with a reel whipped
or tied to the butt end, and a few very large rings at long
intervals up it, to be used in a foul and awkward place with
considerable success, the extra length enabling the angler to
reach holes that he possibly could not get at with a short
trolling rod.   But if there is a considerable clear space over
the weeds and just beyond the reach of the rod point, the
bait can be thrown to the furthest edge of the hole and
worked up and down a few times until it reaches the weeds
that are nearest the rod point, when it must be withdrawn
in the best manner that the circumstances of the place will
allow.   It is the best plan to let a dead gorge plump down
quickly, being careful all the time that the line is tight,
and to lift it back again towards the surface more slowly.
The action of the water, in conjunction with the shape of
the bait, causes it to gyrate more in its upward journey than
it does during its downward plunge.   I have always fancied
that a dead gorge bait looked more natural in the water than
the very best spinning bait I ever mounted, anyhow I know
that a dead gorge, worked as it should be among the weeds,
is the most deadly plan, that can be tried.   When a pike
collars the bait, you must not get excited and strike at once,
or in all probability you will simply jerk it out of his mouth.
A dead gorge must be swallowed; and it all depends on the
humour of a jack as to how long it will take to perform this

operation, he might swallow it within two minutes, or he might be a quarter of an hour. When he runs off with it, ease the line and let him go, don't check him in the slightest, and when he stops allow him five minutes, or maybe eight would be safer, to get it down. If he has swallowed it all right you need not strike, but simply wind him out the best way you can, weeds and all.

I have seen all sorts of hooks and tackle recommended for this job, some of them without the twisted wire, and insteaa of the stiff and rigid lead they are fitted up with a flexible or jointed lead, so that the bait can move about in any direction. I don't recommend any of these, believing that the stiff wire is a protection to the bait when it is dragged through the weeds. It seems to be the usual plan to mount a gorge hook so that when the bait is worked upwards towards the surface the points of those hooks faces the same way, and are liable to catch the weeds during its upward journey. One man who used to do a lot of dead-gorging always used to let his bait plump downwards, tail first, bringing it up again towards the surface, head foremost; that is, exactly reversing the position of the bait from what it would be if worked in the ordinary way. To accomplish this he used to have the twisted wire on his hook very stiff and strong, and exactly long enough to reach from the bottom edge of the gill covers of his bait down to about half an inch from the fork of the tail. In baiting this, instead of running the baiting needle in at the mouth, he used to drive it in close under the gill covers, bringing it out about half an inch or a little less from the root of the tail. After drawing the leaded hook and wire completely through the bait until the points of the hook, or rather the bends of the hook laid on the bottom edge of the gill covers with the points free. He used to again push the needle straight through the root of the tail, and bring it out on the opposite side to where the hooks laid, and again pass it through the bait lengthways, but this time carefully bringing it out of the mouth and drawing the gimp after it. Now, you see by the gimp going in at the gill covers, right down to the tail, and up again to the mouth, the position is reversed, the tail of the bait goes downwards through the water first, and the bends of the hooks faces the weeds, instead of the points, when it is jerked upwards and withdrawn. In this plan it is a necessity to have the wire of the gorge hook pretty long and stiff, and firmly embedded in the solid flesh of the bait, or the wear and tear of dragging it among the weeds would soon rip it all to pieces. I have seen this tackle and plan of baiting used in very deep and open water where no weeds and obstructions exist, instead of a spinning bait, and certainly when the fish laid low and were very sluggish it was more successful than either spinning or live-baiting. It is thrown right across to the opposite side and allowed to sink to the bottom, and then very slowly, inch by inch, wound home again. The bends of the hooks coming first prevented any fouling. This is a deadly plan that I have had proof off more than once; but I say again that I don't like it, because no matter if the fish weighs one pound or twenty pounds, it must be killed when hooked on a dead gorge; but for all that in very deep and open water with a clear bottom it is more deadly than even the paternoster tackle.

CHAPTER VII.

THE PIKE *(continued)*.

FISHING WITH A LIVE BAIT.

Different methods of live baiting—Pike floats and pilots—Snap tackle and the methods of baiting—Traces for live baiting—Stream fishing for pike—The slider float—Striking, and playing a pike on float tackle—The proper depth—A contrast—Live gorging—Paternostering for pike—Legering—Queer live baits—Live bait kettles and store boxes.

Live-baiting for pike can be divided into four heads, or rather sections, two of them practised with one or more floats, and the other two without floats at all; but I don't propose to go at very great length into this part of my subject, describing the dozens of tackles that are recommended for this branch of angling. I shall only briefly look at them from a working man's standpoint, and just see which tackle out of the whole lot is most likely to have the best results when used in any and all circumstances and conditions of live-baiting. The four heads under which live-baiting can be subdivided are as follows:—First, with a snap tackle, and one or more floats so arranged that the bait swims at any depth the angler pleases, mid-water or nearer the bottom or nearer the surface, the snap hooks being such that when the pike seizes the bait he can be struck at once. Second, with similar floats, but with a double side or gorge hook threaded under the skin of the bait, so that a pike must swallow it before he can be hooked. Third, with a paternoster that is used without floats, but has a pear-shaped lead at the extreme end below the baits, and one, two, or sometimes three sets of hooks projecting at right angles from the main trace at fixed distances from each other above the lead. Fourth, with a leger tackle sunk to the bottom of deep holes, with the bait below the lead, and fished as either

a gorge tackle or a semi-gorge snap. Snap fishing with float
tackle is a plan that is now very much in vogue amongst the
anglers who ply their craft on lakes, cuttings, backwaters,
and other quiet waters and rivers that are, comparatively
speaking, free from weeds. Floats themselves are made in
various shapes and sizes, round, long, egg-shaped, and one
that has been registered has the body made like a hollow
cylinder with different coloured tops fitting in like corks, so
that under various aspects of the weather and the lights and
shades that play about on the surface of the water and the
shadows from flags and bushes, the colour of the top could
be altered to suit the eyesight of the angler without having
to remove the whole float.   Various sorts of material are
also used in the manufacture of pike floats, such as wood,
cork, celluloid, etc., etc., and some anglers who cannot afford
to spend much over their sport use a plain bung from an
old barrel with considerable success. Personally I like an
egg-shaped one, with a hole lengthways through the centre,
into which a plug of wood can be fitted, so that when
the line is threaded through this hole the plug holds
it tight in its position at the proper depth.   The
" Fishing Gazette" float is the most useful that can
be tried.   This float has a slit or nick cut down
one side through to the centre plug hole, the object of the
slit being so that the float can be taken off the line and a
larger or smaller substituted, as the case demanded, without
having to undo the knots and take off the tackle.   One
about two and a half inches long down the longest part will
be the most useful general size that can be used, although
it will be necessary some odd times, I daresay, to have one
much larger, or even smaller, for special occasions.   About
a couple of feet or so from the larger float, nearer the rod
point, there is another float, called a pilot. This is generally a much smaller one, and quite round in shape, one
about three-quarters of an inch in diameter being plenty
large enough.   The object of this small float or pilot is to
keep the line on the surface and prevent it from sinking
down and getting mixed up with the bait and tackle; indeed, some anglers that I know when fishing in shallow
water have two pilots a yard or so apart, in addition to the
float proper.

The trace for live-baiting differs slightly from the one recommended for spinning, although the latter will do very well at a pinch. The one most generally in use, however, is a yard length of gimp, or strong salmon gut, with a loop on one end and a No. 4 or 5 buckle swivel on the other. Just above the swivel, threaded on the gimp, is a barrel lead about one and a half or two inches long, and about as thick as a fair sized swan quill. The lead and swivel should be about 14in. from the bait. The main object of the lead is not so much cocking the float, as it is keeping the bait down and preventing it from rising to the surface. In the trace for spinning there are at least two swivels and a drop or hanging lead; in a live-bait trace the buckle swivel fixed at the end is ample, and the lead need only be a plain one, with a hole lengthways down the centre, so that it can be threaded on the gimp or gut.

Snap tackles are now made in almost an endless variety, each one of them claiming to be better than any of the others, the object of the snap tackle being, as its name suggests, snapping or striking the pike directly after he seizes the bait. The best known and the most widely used tackle at the present day is the old-fashioned Jardine snap, which is simply two treble hooks, only one hook that forms each treble is smaller than the other two, fixed a certain distance from each other to suit the size of bait used. Indeed, it is a general plan now to have one of the trebles made with eyes so that it can be shifted closer to the other or further apart to suit the size of bait used. This old tackle holds its

FIG. 12. THE JARDINE SNAP.

own among the many that have since been introduced to supersede it; in fact, in my opinion, none of them are any better, and some of them decidedly not so good. The usual Jardine snap that is generally sold by tackle dealers, has the

small hook of the end treble much too small. I prefer it
at least half the size of the other two, so as to take a good
hold into the root of the shoulder or pectoral fin of the
bait. The accompanying illustration of the Jardine most in
use nowadays shows the small hook of the end treble, no
larger than a roach hook, whereas in my opinion it should
be several sizes larger. Some anglers, Mr. Jardine, I believe, among the number, sometimes fixes this tiny hook
into the gill cover of the bait itself, in which case a small
hook would probably be the best; but I most certainly prefer a larger one and fix it firmly into the root of the shoulder
fin. The moveable treble is fixed in such a place on the
gimp that it can be run fair under the root of the back fin,
taking hold of, at least, a quarter of an inch of solid flesh.
I have seen anglers who did not understand the proper use
of this tackle, fix a bait on it in strange positions, such as
one of the trebles through both lips, and the end one fair
into the sides, or one of the trebles under the back fin and
the other into the root of the tail. This rough sketch shows
the position of the two trebles on the bait, only for the
sake of plain illustration they are pictured much too large,
with the gimp, the shanks of hooks, and the bindings much
too coarse, and the draughtsman has also drawn both hooks
in a straight line, whereas the shank of the top treble should
be pointing straight upwards about level with the top corner
of the dorsal or back fin, instead of so much to the right
hand. But, anyhow, it shows what I consider to be about
the proper position for the hooks to be fixed in the bait in

FIG. 13. METHOD OF BAITING THE JARDINE SNAP.

order to give the best results. Another Jardine tackle is
now made that has a wire fastened to the end treble in
such a manner that it can be threaded in at the mouth and

out at the gill covers, a spiral twist at the end like a cork-screw enabling it to be fastened to the gimp between the two sets of hooks. This spiral wire was made to supersede the small hook of the end treble, the wire holds the bait firmly in its position without sticking the small hook into the shoulder fin, or, indeed, having the small hook there at all. It was claimed for this so-called improvement of the Jardine tackle that a bait could be held much more secure than with an ordinary one, and that it could be hurled long distances in wide lakes or rivers without throwing off. But unfortunately on a careful trial by practical men this long casting was a source of danger and injury to the bait. If the casting was made ever so careful, sometimes the gill cover of the bait would be torn completely away, and even if the bait was only used at close quarters and no damage done to it by long casting, the wire props open the mouth and gill covers, with the result that the bait soon dies and won't work as it should do from the very first; it seems to be cramped and choked, and does not work about as I like to see a live bait work.

FIG. 14. THE WIRED JARDINE SNAP.

Another tackle that used to be a great favourite with us some years ago was a good deal like a Jardine, except the hook that went under the back fin. This was a fair sized moveable single hook, instead of the moveable treble, the end hook being exactly the same in both cases, and the method of baiting identical. The improved Bickerdyke tackle, shown in the accompanying illustration is, according to all reports of my pike fishing customers who have used it, a very good one indeed. The end treble has the small hook reversed with the shank lengthened considerably, the object of this long shanked hook being so that when a pike seizes the bait the hook can be drawn free from the bait, allowing a much better chance of hooking your quarry. The moveable single hook shown in the illustration is stuck firmly under the back fin, the double hook with the long shank reversed hook goes under the skin of the shoulder, so that the two hooks lay on the bait exactly in the position shown for baiting the ordinary "Jardine," and the treble hook that hangs free, is simply put over the bait on the opposite side to the other shoulder hooks and allowed to hang free without being stuck in the bait at all, or the point of one hook can be, if the angler likes, just hanked under the skin towards the belly if he does not like to see it swinging loose, but it may be a source of danger when

FIG. 15. THE BICKERDYKE SNAP.

striking a fish if it is made fast in the bait. There are many more snap tackles made for use with live bait, such as saddle snaps that have two sets of hooks that straddle over the bait, and others too numerous to mention here, all more or less efficient for the work they are made to do; but taking things all round I don't think the old fashioned Jardine can be beaten. The working man pike fisherman, who has not got much money to spare for his tackle, may rest contented very well with them. One of my friends used to bait the Jardine somewhat different to the plan just described, instead of putting the end hook into the root of the shoulder fin, he used to put it fair on the top of the back, close behind the head; he would have it that, with a pike having eyes on the top of his head he was generally looking upwards, and could not see the hooks so well when fixed on the top of the back of the bait. There may be

H

something in this, but I don't think it matters much, as that old friend never had much better luck, and sometimes not so good as I had when adopting the ordinary plan. I don't recommend very large hooks unless the baits are extra big, No. 3 or 4 being ample for all ordinary purposes. For exceptional circumstances, where you know there is a very large pike, and you are trying him with a half-pound bait, or even a small jack which, by the way, is often a splendid bait for those large cannibal pike that inhabit a quiet cutting or isolated pool, it will be as well to have an extra large and strong snap tackle made up with some No. 1 trebles. In snap fishing when the water is only moderately clear, it does not matter so much about the tackle; oo copper gimp will be quite good enough for both trace and tackle, but if the water has run down very fine indeed, then a good strong gut trace will be less visible to the fish. The hooks themselves should be dressed on six or seven inches of gimp, then a single strand of strong salmon gut with a loop at each end, fixed between the gimp of the hooks and the buckle swivel on end of the trace, and finally a two or three feet trace of the strongest gut the angler can afford. Tackle for live livebaiting should always, if possible, be finer than spinning tackle, because in the latter case the bait revolves swiftly through the water, while in the former it is, comparatively speaking, stationary. The best colour for a float would be green with a white top, some anglers like them dark blue with a red top; but a good deal of this is only fancy. In snap fishing down a current that runs into an eddy, it is the best to fix the float so that the bait is some two-thirds of the distance down, that is, within eighteen inches or two feet from the bottom; if this distance can anyhow be guessed, if not, a heavy plummet hung on the buckle swivel and quietly sunk to the bottom will soon tell the proper depth; this mind, is for fishing clear running rivers that have pikey looking corners and eddies, into which a current gurgles and glides, with a bottom, comparatively speaking, clear and free from weeds, and an overhanging row of bushes or sedges lining the side. In this method of snap fishing, fix the small pilot float about a foot above the larger one, for reasons that will be given presently. In live-baiting a quiet lake or similar still water, the pilot is principally used to keep the line on the surface. In stream fishing this does not matter as the line is generally played out from the reel tight, but still a pilot is useful in detecting a proper run from a pike, or only an extra spurt from the bait when he pulls the first float under. In fishing a corner or eddy such as just described, the angler should stand right at the head of the swim, and just drop his bait on the outer edge of the stream, and let it work down the current at the further side of the eddy, letting it go just fast enough to prevent it from being swept too near the bank on which he stands. When the floats reach the eddy proper, by being slightly held back, the bait will work in a semicircular direction round the edge of the eddy towards the bank, and perhaps again take an outward direction towards the centre of the curl, if that eddy is of the shape known to Trent men as an umbrella; pike very often lay on the outer edge of these eddies, just between the sharp current and the curling water. The quieter parts of a streamy river, where a nice little current glides into an eddy and then seems to divide into two, with a wedge shaped pool between, should always be well tried, even if the bait has to be twenty-five or thirty yards away from where you stand. A little careful observation and manipulation of the floats and bait, by being dropped on one of the streams that glides down and across into these wedge shaped eddies, will result in reaching them without much trouble. In live-baiting distant places like that, it is rather difficult to hit the exact depth, and to be right, in my opinion, the bait should be about eighteen inches from the bottom; but the worst of these streams and eddies is the fact that the depth might vary. The best way to try the place is to put the float at what you consider to be the right depth with only the leaded trace, and throw it as near as you can to the spot you wish to fish, if the lead is on the bottom the float will bob about, and you want to be a lot shallower; if, on the other hand, the float rides quietly, you are not deep enough. If after a careful trial you find there is, say, an uniform depth of eight feet, the bait will want to be about six and a half feet from the float, and so on,

always allowing this distance, that is, eighteen inches between the bottom of the river and the bait, no matter how
deep the place is, because I believe in streamy eddies like
those, the jack lay as near the bottom as possible. Sometimes the place may be very deep, say sixteen or eighteen
feet, and you cannot manage very well with a fixed float,
for this you must fish the float as a slider, a good deal after
the plan I described in fishing a deep hole for barbel in
Vol. 1 ; the small pilot can be dispensed with, and instead
of having the larger float with the slit down the side, a
plain one of the same shape will be best. Remove the
plug altogether, so that the float will slip up and down
the line easily, and knot into the line at the right depth a
bit of indiarubber or something similar, of such a size and
shape that it will easily run through the rings on the rod
without jerking or catching, and yet will not go through the
small hole down the centre of the float. In fishing holes
of considerable depth this float drops down the line and
is out of the way of the rod point when the bait is withdrawn ; but when lead and bait sink in the water the float
rises until stopped by the obstruction knotted into the
line. Some anglers may say that places like those could be
much better fished with the paternoster or the ledger tackle,
but I would point out that the character of the streams
down some of these running rivers, between the bank and
the eddies, would be all against ledgering or paternostering ;
the strong current might drown the line and sweep the
bait anywhere but where it was wanted, and a float on the
surface, be the only plan of keeping the bait in the required
position. Another question that anglers don't seem to be
agreed on, is the time that should be allowed between the
jack taking the bait and the striking, when snap fishing ;
this in a great measure depends on the nature of the water
operated on, in stream fishing the pike generally takes a
bait very quickly, and can be struck almost immediately.
In lake or still water fishing the pike seem to me to be
much more deliberate in their actions, and should be
allowed a few seconds, say five or six, after the float dis-
appears. In the stream fishing that we have just now
been discussing, and the bait is of a fair size and lively, the

float will now and again bob clean under, making the inexperienced think he has got a run ; it was for this purpose of
detecting a good run that I recommended the bait to be
some eighteen inches from the bottom, and the small float
or pilot about a foot from the larger one. As soon as ever
both floats disappear under the surface, and sometimes they
will follow one another like a flash, the line can be tightened
with a slight jerk. Heavy striking is not necessary in this
snap fishing, in fact, it is to be condemned ; you see, when
fishing in this manner down the streams and eddies you have
rod in left hand with finger on edge of reel, and the line,
comparatively speaking, tight between the finger and thumb
of the right hand. A good run from a pike could very
often be felt before it was even seen. If the finger is
pressed tight on the edge of reel, and the point of the rod
raised smartly, the plunge of the hooked fish would be quite
sufficient to drive the hooks well home, without risking a
broken line by striking heavily at a large pike when making his first plunge. If the place has a clear bottom and
is free from obstructions, it is an easy matter to play the
hooked fish, easing the pressure slightly on the edge of reel
as he runs, and winding in whenever you have a chance,
taking care, however, that the line is always taut ; always
play a pike as heavily as you can, and don't allow him to
run all over the place more than you can possibly help.
If it is an awkward place, full of weeds and obstructions,
you will have to be guided by the circumstances of the
case, as to how you play him, but keep him away from
danger at any cost by putting on all the pressure the tackle
will bear, and with a little luck he will be yours. In snap-
fishing with a float in a lake or very quiet river, the bait
cannot be manipulated into the eddies and streams like it
is in stream fishing, you can only throw it out and wait for
a run, of course, winding in a yard of line every now and
again until the bait travels across the open water from the
full extent of the cast, unto nearly the rod point, but each
place will have to be fished according to its own peculiarities. It is a good plan sometimes when fishing a lake or
other sheet of water that has a lot of reed beds all round
the margin, to take a boat, if one is handy, and kick up a

good big row by splashingapole right in the middle of those
reed beds. Large jack very often lay hidden deep among
those reeds, and it is just possible you may startle them out
and into the open water beyond, where later on they would
have a much better chance of seeing one of your baits
than they would while in the middle of that fortress.
This dodge has scored more than once during my experience. A live bait can be thrown a considerable distance
without injury; a gentle swing from the rod point in the
manner described in Chap. 3, being sufficient to get out
thirty yards without jerking the bait from the hooks; but
a live bait on snap tackle must be carefully thrown. In
snap fishing with a live bait the line should always be well
greased, so that in still water it will float on the surface—many a fish has been lost by having a sunk
line between the floats and rod point. Another
point of interest to the would-be pike fisherman is
whether the live bait should be near the bottom, or nearer
the surface; my own opinion and experience favours the
former, especially in deep, quiet waters. If the place is
twelve or fourteen feet deep, I always found it to be the best
to have the bait within a couple of feet of the bottom at
the outside, that is if you wanted the larger fish. During
the winter time they are, as a rule, much too sluggish to
rise up to within three feet of the surface to take a bait; a
few small ones may be got, but the larger ones lie low as a
rule, and like the immortal Mr. Micawber, wait patiently for
something to turn up. Another point is whether a large
bait or a small one is the best, and here again the peculiarities of each place must decide the matter. If the jack only
run small, then a dace from two to three ounces will be
quite large enough; but if the place is a deep, quiet lake,
tenanted by very large pike, then taking things all round
large baits will stand the best chance. Once I remember
getting a fourteen pounder on a dace that only weighed
half an ounce; but the balance of opinion favours the large
bait taking one time with another. I had a very curious
illustration of these last two points some time ago: A
gentleman got a day in a private lake, that was strictly preserved, and only occasional leave granted; the lake swarmed

with pike of all sizes. He fished all day in deep water with the bait (small dace averaging two ounces each), about a yard from his float, and successfully landed ten fish weighing altogether forty-one pounds, largest 5¾lbs. Another gentleman whose ticket was dated for a week later, took down a can of dace that must have gone on the average half-a-pound each; he fished deep down, and landed nine fish weighing altogether 132½lbs., the largest 24½lbs, the smallest 7lbs; a vast difference, which could only be satisfactorily explained by the different methods the two anglers had of going to work, as the conditions were similar on both days. If the place is in a very awkward position and weeds are pretty plentiful, but not sufficient to stop a bait from working about at all, it will be as well to use a live gorge tackle instead of a snap; the hooks of the latter might catch among the weeds, whereas the gorge hook lies flatter on the side of bait, and is less conspicuous. The live gorge is simply a double hook, whipped firmly on the end of a foot or so of fine gimp, and threaded until the hooks lie on the side, close up to the gill covers; the loop of the gimp being brought out just behind the dorsal or back fin. Care must be taken in threading the bait that the needle and gimp only just goes under the skin, and that the points of the hook project well above the side, and are not buried in the bait at all. The same trace and float will do for this as for snap-fishing, the only difference in using a gorge bait, is that the pike must be allowed five or six minutes to swallow the bait, instead of striking at the disappearance of the floats. When the pike seizes the gorge bait you must let him go where he likes, even if he threads right through a bed of weeds, don't check him in the slightest, but pay out line until he stops, and then quietly lay down the rod in such a position that he can take more line off the reel if he wants it, and wait five or six minutes. If before this time expires the float comes to the surface, you may know he has rejected the bait, but if it keeps down unless it gets fast among the weeds, you may hope that he has got it swallowed, and tighten on him, extricating him from among the weeds in the best manner you can. I don't like gorge fishing at all, but still it is useful under some circumstances. A live bait can be worked by it among the weeds much better than with a snap. The bait can be hurled much further without so much danger of throwing off; and, finally, when a pike is fairly hooked, the hooks are down its belly, and not hanging from its jaws to catch in every weed-bed that comes handy. The pike fishermen of the Welsh Harp almost always use a gorge tackle, the main reason for this being that the lake is very shallow, as a rule, all round the margin, and it is necessary to throw out a considerable distance from the bank in order to get any depth of water. The generality of these men have an addition to the ordinary live gorge hook, in the shape of a small wire hook about as big as a little roach hook, but without either point or barb, that is brazed at the back of the other two, and projecting slightly above them. After the hook is threaded in its proper position this very small back hook drops into the hollow under the edge of the gill cover, and takes firm hold of the hard gristle just there. This prevents the gimp from tearing away the skin when the tremendous long casts are made.

Paternostering is another very quiet and deadly method of taking pike, particularly large pike that live in holes and eddies, where the bottom of the river is very unequal in depth. The paternoster is simply a long trace of strong gut or gimp, with a fairly heavy pear-shaped lead at the extreme end, and one or more sets of hooks at intervals higher up. Personally, I consider one set of hooks plenty to use on a paternoster, and this should be fixed at least two feet above the lead. There are various methods of making a paternoster, the most common being a main line about four feet long, with two single sneck bend hooks fixed by bone runners about a foot from each other on the main line. These single hooks are on separate bits of gimp and project about seven inches from the gimp of the main trace. These single hooks are just put through both lips of the live bait, so that when a pike takes them, he must have time given him to get the whole lot in his mouth before he can be hooked. I don't think this single hook is sufficient. The way I made my paternoster was to get a length of good fine gimp for slightly clouded water, and a length of strong gut for very clear water, each about one and a half yards long. A good fair sized and well whipped loop is made at each end, one loop being to fasten the lead in, and the other for the reel line to be attached to. About two feet from the bottom loop a swivel was put in, one of those swivels that has an extra eye or ring projecting at right angles from its side. Into the eye the seven or eight inches of gimp on which the hooks were whipped is attached, swinging clear as it were from the main gut line, the swivel allowing the bait to go round and round the trace without twisting himself up with it.

If the angler uses gut for the main line of his trace, which, I may add, is better for very clear water than gimp. I don't know that it matters about using the very expensive salmon gut, very strong barbel legering gut will do, because it is a dead certainty that the same gut that will kill a 10 or 12lb. barbel will kill almost any pike we are likely to get hold of nowadays.

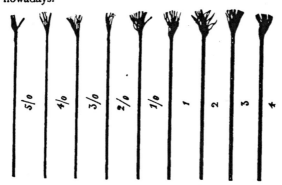

FIG. 16. SIZES OF GIMP.

The hooks should always be dressed on fine copper gimp or twisted flexible wire, it does not matter much which. A short length of very thick and stiff gut is also a very good thing to dress paternoster hooks on. I like a double hook with a small rider brazed at the back, a good deal like the hook of a Jardine snap, at the end of the gimp firmly whipped on, and a little distance above it a

single moveable lip hook of a fair good size, say a No. 1 or
2.   The double hook need not be very large, No. 4 or 5
being plenty big enough.   In baiting this tackle the lip
hook is shifted to suit the size of bait, so that when that
lip hook is through both lips of the bait, the small hook at
the back of the double one reaches to the root of the back
fin, into which it is firmly stuck.   This tackle enables a pike
to be struck as soon as he runs off with the bait, and is
much safer than the single hook only.   In using a paternoster it is necessary to have a tight line, so as to be always
ready when a pike attacks the bait, and work it into all sorts
of eddies and corners, sometimes swinging it out like a pen-
dulum to the far side of the river or open water, allowing
the lead to rest on the bottom, and bringing it inch by inch
to the bank on which you stand.   In fact, it is in almost an
endless variety of ways that a paternoster can be worked;
holes can be tried where any other plan could hardly be
adopted, open spaces among boughs and flags, eddies at the
tail-end of a mill.   You can hardly be wrong anywhere
where jack are to be found, with a paternoster; but it is a
question of practise and experience alone that will make a
successful paternosterer.   I might add that under no circumstances do I like a pike paternoster to have more than one
set of hooks.

   Legering for pike is another plan that, like the paternoster, requires no float, but is, during certain conditions of
the water, a most deadly style to try.   When a heavy flood
or a break-up of the winter's frost causes a strong flush of
water to come down the river, and it clears away sufficiently
to see the bait when sunk a yard below the surface, then is
the time to try the leger in the deep and quiet stretches away
from the main current.   Indeed, in some very deep and
quiet rivers that have a gravelly and level bottom, the leger
is as good a piece of tackle as can be tried.   I like a fair
sized bullet for my leger, one at least an ounce in weight,
with a hole drilled through it sufficiently large to allow the
line to pass easily through.   This bullet is threaded on the
line itself, with a bit of a stop, either a split shot pinched
on, or a little bit of wood half an inch in length, and as
thick as a match half-hitched in the line below it.   This pre-

vents the bullet from dropping down the trace and getting
too near the bait. The proper distance between bullet and
bait is about three and a half feet. Below the bullet, joined
to the line, is a trace of either gimp or gut, with a small
long barrel lead on it, and a buckle swivel at the end. The
lead, as just noted, should be as thin as possible, say about
one and a half inches long and no thicker than a goose quill,
so that when a jack runs off with the bait the lead is no
obstruction to him. Below the lead and buckle swivel is
the tackle, and this can either be a double gorge hook or
the tackle recommended in paternoster fishing. A tackle
that I used to use sometimes in the deep waters of the Ouse,
was an ordinary gorge tackle with the gimp threaded
under the skin and brought out behind the back fin in the
usual way, and an extra gorge hook mounted on a very short
loop of gimp not more than a quarter of an inch long, with
a very small hook whipped at the back. The eye or loop
of this extra double hook was dropped over the gimp on
the main tackle and brought right down to the back fin of
the bait, and the tiny hook at back just stuck under the
skin. This extra hook then laid flat to the side, and was
not so liable to catch any obstruction on the bottom of river
as the ordinary treble snap hooks. When a pike takes this
tackle you can venture to strike or tighten him nearly as
quick as snap fishing, the hanging hooks in the centre are
bound to take hold if the pike gets the bait in his mouth at
all. Anyhow, when you get a run, I should not allow him
to go more than a couple or three yards before tightening
on him. If you use an ordinary gorge tackle for legering,
when you have to give the fish time to swallow the bait,
you should see that the line can be easily drawn through the
bullet, so that any amount of line can be taken off the reel
without the bullet shifting at all. Every knot, loop, etc.,
on the line or tackle should be between the bullet and the
bait. The long barrel lead that is on the trace some 18
inches above the bait is merely used as a weight to keep it
from running too far about and getting so far away from the
leger bullet. About 14 or 15 inches from the bait; in fact,
close up to the buckle swivel of the trace, between it and
the long barrel lead, it will be as well to put a rough bit

of cork, any old bottle cork will do cut in half, with a nick in the flat side, into which the gimp can be stuck. This bit of cork will help the bait to swim some few inches above the bottom, and be more attractive than if the weight of tackle kept him flat on his side at the bottom.

1362

FIG 17. DISGORGING SCISSORS.

I think I have said as much as I need say about live-baiting for pike; hooking and playing the fish have been carefully considered in another part of this volume; but I might just mention a peculiar thing that has often come under my notice, and that is that the pike of almost any river or stream prefers a live bait from a strange river in preference to those taken from the same stream in which he lives. It may be fancy, but a can of Thames dace seemed to be more attractive to the Ouse pike than baits taken from the latter river; while Trent dace were liked by Witham jack, and vice versa. I don't know if there is anything in this, but still during my career as a professional several like cases have cropped up that have been, to say the least, very peculiar. Pike are sometimes caught with very queer live baits, the two most noteworthy instances that

came under my own observation were a small jack over a
pound in weight, and a live blackbird with a broken wing.
In the former case we knew that a large pike tenanted a
pool some little distance from the Trent, but all efforts to
catch him by the ordinary baits proved futile. At last a
well-known Newark tradesman tried him with a small jack
that weighed at least a pound and a quarter. This fish was
threaded on a very large gorge tackle, and for nearly an hour
lugged four or five large live bait floats about manfully round
and round that pool. At last he took it, and we gave him
half an hour to swallow the bait, which he did. We
were disappointed over that fish, it was no less than 45 inches
long, and only scaled up to 16lb. The other case was also
in a pool away from the main river. We had noticed earlier
in the day a jack make a grab at a yellow wagtail that sat on
the edge of a weed bed. A small terrier we had with us
found a wounded blackbird with a broken wing under the
hedge bottom. This bird we carefully tied on a saddle
tackle, so that one set of hooks was on its back and the
other under its breast. Removing the trace, lead, and floats
this bait was thrown out like a huge fly. He flopped on the
water, making a rare commotion for a minute or so, when a
5lb. jack snatched him under and was safely landed. That
was the only time I ever fished with a live bird for a bait,
and I did not feel at all proud of the exploit, as it was a
cold-blooded job, to say the very best; but the pike snapping at the wagtail, and the dog finding the wounded bird
so soon afterwards, gave us a hint. But it was a strange
thing, as we had tried the same pool dozens of times before
and never landed a jack on a live fish out of it. Once I
got a brace of jack when chub fishing with a lump of pith,
and a friend of mine one afternoon landed four when bream
fishing with worms. A live bait kettle is also a necessity
of the pike fisherman as a receptacle to carry his live baits
about in. I have seen all sorts in use, from a square bis-
cuit tin with a string handle, to Field's patent can, that has
an arrangement fixed to it to pump air among the water.
The accompanying illustration show the kinds that are generally in use; but perhaps the best of the lot is the one that
has an inner kettle of perforated zinc that can be lifted in

and out of the outer one. This arrangement is useful in a
variety of ways, for one thing the baits can be got at without

FIG. 18. LIVE BAIT KETTLES.

putting the hand into the cold water—a consideration when
the weather is nippingly cold—and another thing, the inner
kettle can be set in the stream with the main stock of baits,
so as to freshen them up if they got weak and sickly by
being carried about too long.   If the angler lives close to
the water it would be as well to keep a stock of baits by him
if he possibly can.   The best thing is a strong hamper that
has a closely fitting lid.   Some men have a wooden box or
trunk with a wire grating at each end, and the bottom and
lid perforated plentifully with half-inch holes.   In my
opinion, based on a long experience with both, I am decidedly in favour of the wicker one sunk to the bottom, as
the baits keep longer and in better condition in it than in a
wooden one floating just under the surface.   One of the

best things I ever saw to keep live baits in was a stone trough
that was fixed under a pump at the bottom of an old friend's
garden. This trough was made out of a peculiar red sand
stone, and had been there in all probability a good many
years. It did not matter how sickly and weak the baits
were when turned out of the can, they soon recovered in the
trough. Perhaps there was some virtue or other in the old
stone, anyhow I never knew any other pump trough that
would keep baits so long and so well. I might also just tell
the novice that it is not a good plan to keep live baits all
night in a small bait can, as he would be bound to find
some of them dead in the morning, and the rest not very
lively. If you have nothing else, put them in a good sized
pail with a landing net over the top, and let a tap drip into
them all night; if no tap is available, use a good big tub
three parts filled with water. A lump of ice put on the lid
of a can will sometimes keep the baits alive for many hours.

Before I close this chapter I might just say that good silk
gimp is better for pike traces than the twisted steel wire that
is sometimes recommended. The latter is finer, and shows
less in the water, but it will occasionally kink, and when it
does kink it snaps very easily. Short lengths of twisted
wire are extremely useful to dress the hooks of snap, etc.,
tackles on; but when a long trace is required I strongly
advise either gimp or gut, for the reason just stated. Wire
will kink and break very easily—at least this is my experience.

I think I have said as much as I need say on the subject
of pike fishing that is likely to be of interest to the working
man angler. Fishing with such items as a pike fly, or an
artificial rat, or the thousand and one different tackles and
artificials that are now put on the market would only be a
slight variation not worth mentioning. The general principles I lay down in the foregoing pages would be the same
in nearly all instances.

CHAPTER VIII.

THE PERCH.

PERCH AND PERCH FISHING.

The veteran and his first perch—Habits and haunts of perch—Perch packing in the winter—A cruel slaughter—Description of the perch— Weight of perch—" His eyes bigger than his belly "—Perch in the frying pan—Rod, reel, line, and tackle for perch fishing—Stream fishing for perch—Paternostering—Float fishing with a minnow—Fly fishing—Artificial baits for perch.

I find that I have gone into the subject of pike fishing at such a length that the space left at my disposal to treat of perch and perch fishing is only very limited, so I must be as brief as I possibly can in this chapter, only laying down the principal rules that must guide the novice who wishes to practice this branch of angling.

. I wonder how many grey-haired veterans among the vast army of Britain's anglers who, looking back over a career spent by the side of river, lake, pond, and stream, cannot say that it was the capture of a small perch or two in some pond or canal that was the starting point of their angling experi-ences, and so fired them with enthusiasm for the sport that they have stuck to it till unable to get down to the water-side, and can now only sit by the fire and think of all the glorious days they have had since those boyhood's times, when the first perch snatched down their float so startlingly sudden that it nearly upset their nerves. There is no fish better adapted than small perch, that live in a pond or canal, to start a boy on his angling experiences. This class of perch is not particular what sort of tackle it is, neither does he care much about the bait—a worm freshly dug out of the garden, a slug picked at random from the cabbage bed, or a bunch of green and stinking gentles will all be greedily swallowed. And then again it does not matter about accurately plumbing the depth, or carefully ground-baiting a swim, or any one of the hundreds of minute details that go towards making, say, roach fishing such a fine art.

"Yes," some of you may say, "this is all very well talking about those ill-fed and hungry pond perch taking anything that is offered them, but what about a good well-fed river perch, that has a plentiful supply of small fry knocking about next door to him, as it were?" As the old saying goes, "this is a horse of another colour." A boy with a bent pin, a thick bit of gut, a heavy lead, and a rough home-made float, won't make much impression on him, he might catch one or two by accident during certain conditions of the water; but, say, during August, September, and October, when the rivers have run down very clear and bright, and even the knots on the tackle can be plainly seen deep down in the water, Mr. Perch is a particular wide-awake customer. To get them then you have to be as an old friend of mine put it, "as artful as a waggon-load of monkeys." You have got to use fine tackle, and you will have to use it far off. The bait also will have to be delicate and attractive, and mounted on the hooks in the most careful manner. During the early part of the season, that is, latter end of June and the first two or three weeks of July, perch are not quite so careful as they are a little later on. At that time they will very often take the small red worm or the cad baits when dace fishing down the shallow streams or run at a small artificial minnow. Just at that time they are picking up after spawning and cleaning, but a month or two later, when well fed and in good condition, they leave the shallow streams and seek refuge in deeper water, under the roots and hollows of an overhanging bank, in the deep and quiet eddies, round about the woodwork of an old bridge, in the deep and strong waters by the side of flags and rushes, and in the deep eddies by the side of the swirling water from a weir. It is then during the late summer and autumn that the big ones take some catching. The very worst time for poor Mr. Perch is after a sharp winter, when the ice and frost have broken up, and the river is tearing down in high flood. At this time they pack themselves together in large numbers, seeking the quiet corners, eddies, and even deep

I

dyke ends, out of the way of the raging flood water. Poor
fellows, they have been most likely on very short commons
during the long cold winter, and as a consequence very sharp
set. When the water clears a little, and the angler drops
across a corner in which a large shoal is packed, the execu-
tion is sometimes pitiful. A few handfuls of chopped-up
worms are thrown in, and a red worm on the hook; and
sometimes the sport (save the mark) continues until every
perch is cleared out of the hole. Once only I can remember
being in at the death of a whole shoal of packed perch, and
even now I feel a little bit ashamed of the exploit. I found
them at home in a deep hole at a dyke end that ran into
the River Witham, not very far from where the county of
Lincoln joined the county of Nottingham. It was during
the early days of February, just after the frost of a long
and severe winter had broken up, and the yellow flood-
water was tearing down the river in high spate. A few yards
up the dyke the water was, comparatively speaking, clear,
and at least seven or eight feet deep. In about three hours
I had landed three dozen fair good perch weighing a little
over 20lb., and considered I had cleared every one out of
the hole, as during the remainder of the afternoon I failed
to add a single one to the bag. I have heard of as many
as 200 being taken at one sitting under similar circumstances; but, thank goodness, whatever may have been my
piscatorial sins, I have not one of that magnitude to answer
for.

The perch is a member of the Percidæ family, and is a
representative of the spinous-finned fish, that is, having
spikes or prickles on the end of the rays of some of his
fins. A great characteristic of this fish is the second fin on
the back. His scientific name is Perca Fluviatilis, and he
is a very handsome, well-made member of the finny tribe;
in fact, I consider him a gem of the first water. Look at
the beautiful scarlet of his fins, the golden rings of his eyes,
the pale green of his sides, shaded and relieved by the
darker bars that stripe his body from the shoulder to the
tail. His scales are small, very hard, and extremely difficult to scrape off, but they are arranged in such perfect
order; in fact, he appears to me to be about as perfect a

fish form as it is possible to conceive. The dark stripes or bars down each side of this fish number, I think, never more than seven, although I have one here set up that has nine down one side; but I fancy this was only a lark of the preserver, who fancied he could improve on Nature.

Perch spawn early, say by the latter end of April or the beginning of May, and they choose peculiar positions for this operation. They deposit their ova on the submerged boughs, just under the surface of the water, and on the reed weed and flag beds, and sometimes over the stones on the shallows, spreading the ova all over everything handy, like long festoons of lace. Swans, ducks, and other water-fowl reap a merry harvest at this time, for nothing could be handier for them than perch spawn, which they speedily gobble up by the yard. Perch are wonderfully prolific, as many as three quarters of a million of eggs have been calculated to be in the ovum of a pound fish; and so there stands need to be, for perch spawn stands a very poor chance of coming to maturity, in all probability not more than one egg out of every thousand reaches the fish stage. This fish in favourable and well preserved waters will reach a very fair size, odd ones have been taken that exceeded 4lb. I should say that four and a half pounds would be the very outside weight of this fish in British waters. We have heard of English perch reaching the extraordinary weight of six, eight, and even one of nine pounds, but there does not appear to be any evidence in existence that such can now be seen preserved, so I am afraid we must take these gigantic perch with a good deal of caution. A two pounder is a good one, while as for a three pounder, they are not often caught. I have seen them taken from various rivers when they tipped the beam at from two to two and a half pounds, and probably twice when they scaled nearly three pounds; but never yet have I landed one or seen one landed that went over the three pounds. In some of the Scandinavian lakes we hear of them reaching extraordinary dimensions, and in the Danube there are some that go into the teens of pounds. The perch is blessed, or perhaps he would call it cursed with a very large mouth, and sometimes it is wonderful the bait he will go for, he must regulate the size of his

quarry by the size of his mouth, and not by the size of his
stomach at all, for some odd times it would be an utter im-
possibility for him to swallow the bait he ran at. The most
extraordinary case that I ever heard off, was a little perch
of only five or six ounces running at and getting hooked on
a gigantic spoon, that a friend had purchased to use for
large pike in one of the Irish lakes. He laid the fish in
the bowl of the spoon, like a herring on a dish; whatever
that perch took a six inch spoon to be, is merely a matter
of speculation. I have taken half and three quarter
pounders on pike baits, that it was utterly impossible for
him to swallow; they seemed to me to be like the boy in
the nursery rhyme, whose eyes were bigger than his belly.
As a fish for the table perch are A 1, being remarkably firm,
white, and sweet in the flesh. It is not much good trying
to scrape the scales off; the best plan to prepare them for
the table is to cut off the head, tail, and fins, remove the
insides, and wash them well inside and out, dry them
thoroughly with a cloth and drop them in a frying pan
among a liberal supply of boiling lard. As soon as they
are cooked sufficiently on one side turn them over, and re-
peat the dose on the other. The skin and scales will all
slip off together as soon as the cooking is completed. I
am wonderfully fond of a dish of good river perch, and
consider them better than a good fresh haddock, and equal
to a lemon sole. With regard to the rod, reel, line, and
tackle necessary for perch fishing, there is no need for anything very special, except an odd item or two, for extraordinary purposes. A good strong roach rod, eleven feet
long, or a decent chub rod with an extra short top for occasional spinning, will be plenty good enough without running to the expense of a special rod for perch. The reel
also can be a plain, easy going Nottingham, three and a
half inches in diameter, or the centre pin reel I so carefully
described in the vol. on barbel and chub fishing. The
line also can be the stout roach or the chub line, say a
No. 7 or No. 6 at the outside, and of undressed plaited silk,
in fact, you cannot do better than use the rod, reel, and
line I describe in Vol. I for chubbing down the streams.
Perch tackle should be fairly fine, I don't recommend the

very finest, four or five x drawn gut for stream fishing, although it should not be any stouter than the finest refina,
undrawn quality. Hooks should be nearly as large as recommended for chub, say, Nos. 6, 7, and 8, and they can
either be round bends, crystals, or sneck bends, according
to fancy or the bait in use. Floats can be swan quill, some
six or seven inches long, capable of carrying half-a-dozen
B.B. split shot for use down lighter streams, and a pelican
quill or small Nottingham curved cork float, capable of
carrying ten to a dozen shots for work down the deeper,
heavier waters. A small pilot, say about three quarters of
an inch in diameter, a good deal like the one recommended
in live-baiting for pike, will also be extremely useful in
fishing the holes under the boughs or roots with a single
minnow. Tackle for worm fishing need not be much longer
than a yard, anyhow, I should say a gut line a yard long with
a loop at each end, and stained either a dark blue or a yel-
lowish brown will be capable of fishing nearly any place
that contains perch. Hooks to suit all purposes can be
carried securely whipped to fine single lengths of gut
stained the same colour as the main gut line. By having
your hook lengths separate, you can easily change the hook
should a different size or pattern be required for special
baits or purposes. The food of perch consists principally
of the small fry of most sorts of fresh-water fish. Although
he will take worms of various sorts, from a huge lobworm
down to a tiny cockspur; I look upon him as being a fish
eater generally. Nor is he by any means confined to worms
and small fish, for he will sometimes go for a lump of cheese
paste intended for a chub, a bit of bread crust when roach
fishing, or a bunch of gentles or cad-baits when fishing the
streams for dace, and even when raking the bottom for
gudgeon perch will take the tiny scrap of worm intended
for the smaller fish. But still, as I said before, I don't
look upon those baits as being his staple food. I have
dozens of times seen large perch on the feed, he gets on
the track of a bleak, chasing it right across the river and
all over the place, all the time close to the surface, chopping at it with a splash a dozen or more times until the
poor bleak gets too exhausted to jump for freedom any

more, it is almost sure to fall a victim at last, as I never yet
saw a bleak in the deep, quiet stretches of the Ouse succeed
in escaping from a perch, and I have watched the contests
some scores of times. I don't know as I need say anything
about fishing down the streams for perch with a worm, except that the worm, be it the tail end of a lob or the suc-
culent marsh worm, or the red cockspur, should be clean
and well scoured, and swum down very near the bottom,
and let the swims be as long as possible, for it is a good
deal like roach fishing when water is clear; fine and far
off must be the order of the day. The instructions given
for roach fishing down the streams in Vol. 2 will fit in for
perch fishing exactly; a few scraps of clipped up worms
thrown in from time to time in the track of the float is all
that is required by way of ground bait. The only difference between roach and perch fishing in this style, and in
the summer and autumn months, is that in roaching we
generally stick to one place during the day, especially if it
is a well ground-baited swim, whereas in perch fishing it is
the best to rove about, throwing a few scraps of ground-
bait into every fresh place tried. A small fish, say a minnow or a tiny gudgeon, in fact, anything not over two inches
long, will be found as good as anything that can be tried
during the autumn months, and these can be fished on
either a float tackle or a paternoster. The most common
paternoster in use is generally made of stout gut, with a
couple of bone runners at intervals in it; fastened to these
bone runners are single sneck bend hooks dressed on short
lengths of pig's bristles, while at the bottom is a pear shaped
lead of a size to suit the requirements of the stream. Some
anglers say that nothing else is so good as pig's bristles to
dress the hooks on, as they always stick out straight from
the main gut line at right angles, whereas a bit of gut col-
lapses and hangs downwards. I don't know, I am sure,
because I never used a bristle in my life; I always found
a bit of stiff gut, about four inches long, plenty good
enough for me. The way I like a paternoster to be made,
is to have a gut line, fairly fine, about one and a half yards
long, with a couple of those swivels (very small size, with an
extra eye in the side, same as recommended in the chapter

on pike fishing), about eighteen inches from each other,
the bottom swivel to be eighteen inches above the lead.
Into each of these swivels a stiff bit of gut, somewhat
thicker than the main line, is firmly whipped in such a
manner that they stick out at right angles; a bit of gut
about five inches long for each will do very well. On one
of these bits of gut a single round bend hook is whipped on
the extreme end for worms or similar baits; some anglers
only use a single hook for minnows, but I don't consider
it hardly sufficient. I like a tiny treble, one of the smallest
that is made whipped on the end, and a moveable lip hook
several sizes larger, say a No. 8 single, above it. In baiting
a minnow or tiny gudgeon, the moveable lip hook is put
through both lips of the bait, and the tiny treble is stuck
fair into the root of the tail, just where the flesh ends and
the tail fin begins. By having the lip hook moveable, it
can be adjusted to suit any sized bait. In using a small fish
on a single hook baited through both lips, you are obliged
to give a perch time to get it well into his mouth, or you
will fail to hook him. A perch generally seizes his prey
by the tail, and so by having a treble fixed there you can
safely tighten on him, as soon as you feel the first pluck.
Don't use a large treble that looks so awkward and clumsy
against the bait's tail, but get the smallest you can; you
may lose one or two runs by failing to hook firmly with
the little hook, but then, on the other hand, you get more
bites. I like one hook for minnows on my paternoster, and
the other for worms; the bottom one, in my opinion, is
the best for the former, and the top one for the latter. The
lead on the end of the paternoster should be no larger than
you can comfortably swing out, say fifteen yards on the
fine line you are using, and should be worked or dropped
into every available space in which you think a perch is
lurking; if the place is open water and fairly deep, swing
the lead and baits out as far as you can and allow it to
touch the bottom, pause a few seconds, and then raise the
rod point, winding in a foot of line, and so on until you
have searched all the water between the furthest extent of
your cast and the rod point. But whatever you do, don't
let the baits go down too deep, only let the lead rest on

the bottom and always keep the line as tight as possible.
All sorts of places can be searched by a paternoster, but
more particularly those places where the stream is deep and
strong, with a clear and wide expanse of water.   When fishing among the roots and under the boughs I prefer a float
tackle with only one set of hooks on, and this float can
either be a stout pelican quill or a small Nottingham cork,
or the little pilot as before mentioned.   Three or four fair
sized shots are distributed on the tackle at intervals, the
lowest one a foot or so from the hook.   For hooks themselves I have a preference for the same as described on the
paternoster, and baited exactly the same way.   The float
tackle is arranged so as to suit the depth of water, but I
should say if you can anyway hit it, if the bait is a foot to
18in. above the bottom, you stand the best chance.   The
minnow is swum down by the edge of the boughs, or quietly
insinuated into any opening large enough among the roots,
and the draw or strike should be made as soon as you feel
the first pluck of the fish.

FIG. 19. THE DEVON MINNOW.

One of the best day's perch fishing I ever had was down
the Witham, fishing the boughs in this manner.   I got
fifteen perch going nearly a pound apiece on the average,
and three very decent chub, besides losing a few owing to
some very awkward places I tried in: A very simple plan
of carrying live minnows down to the river is by putting
them in a bottle among some clean cold water, one of those
sodawater bottles " without a bottom," as Andy called them,
is as good as anything that can be employed; a half-pint
bottle will accommodate two dozen minnows very well.
Cork them down and slip the bottle in your side pocket;
they will live very well corked down in a bottle.   I suppose

the jolting about during carriage keeps the water well
aerated; but still if two or three small triangular nicks are
cut into the cork, the chances of them living longer will be
all the better. It is a nuisance carrying a bait-can with a

FIG. 20. THE QUILL MINNOW.

few minnows in, a bottle is far handier, you are not so liable
to empty the water into your pocket as you are with a can.
Small perch are sometimes taken with an artificial fly. A
little Zulu with a red tag appears to be the favourite; but
it is very little good, or, indeed, I should suppose hardly
any anglers go after perch specially with the fly. When they
are captured it is generally when dace fishing across the
shallows and streamy backwaters, and looked upon as
merely an accident; but still I have known as many as a
dozen perch to be landed during a single evening on the
fly.

With regard to spinning for perch, this, in my opinion,
is only a very sorry business, and not so safe as either worm
fishing or paternostering. It is true a few odd ones are
got now and again by that plan, but this game is apt to be

FIG. 21. THE SPIRAL MINNOW.

a little expensive. You are in all probability using an artificial that cost from one to two shillings, and small jack will
persist in running at them and quietly severing the gut with
their teeth, and if this happens two or three times during

a day, why the game is hardly worth the candle. It is as well where small jack abound to have four or five inches of fine gimp close up to the swivel of the minnow, or whatever else you are using. Almost any small artificial from one to two inches long will do for perch, such as spoons, Devons, phantoms, spirals, Caledonians, etc., and once I saw a spinning arrangement on which a lob worm was fixed. This, I fancy, was named "The Jigger," and was a pretty fair success. I give here two or three illustrations of arti-

FIG. 22. THE PHANTOM MINNOW.

ficials that are about as good as anything that can be tried for perch, but I say again that it is not a very brilliant plan to fill a bag with large perch.

I must now bring this part of my experiences and instructions to a close, and trust I have made myself perfectly understood, so that no one, however inexperienced, who is anxious to learn, can possibly make a mistake.

LaVergne, TN USA
17 June 2010
186507LV00003B/24/P